AL-GHUNYA LI-TALIBI TARIQ AL-HAQQ

Sufficient Provision for Seekers of the Path of Truth

Shaikh Abdul Qadir Jilani
(May Allah be pleased with him)

Tr. By: Shaikh Muhammad ibn Yahya at-Tadifi al-Hanbalion

KITAB BHAVAN
New Delhi - 110 002 (INDIA)

Name of the Book : Al-Ghunya li Talibi al-Haqq: Sufiicient Provision For Seekers of the path of Truth

Written by : Shaikh Abdul Qadir Jilani

Translated by : Shaikh Muhammad ibn Yahya at-Tadifi al-Hanbalion

Reprint : 2021

ISBN-10 : 81-7151-392-1
ISBN-13 : 978-81-7151-392-5

Book Code No. : A00073

Batch ID : IVRY21062021

Printed & Published in India by : Moonis Ali Nasri for KITAB BHAVAN
1784, Kalan Mahal, Darya Ganj,
New Delhi - 1100 02 [India]

PRINTED IN INDIA

If you have any corrections, comments. or questions about this publication, please feel free to contact us.

CONTENTS

Author's Prologue..4

Concerning knowledge of the Creator [Sani'] (Almighty and Glorious is He)..7

Concerning contentment [rida]..24

Concerning absolute trust in the Lord [tawakkul]...............39

Concerning thankfulness [shukr]...53

A series of invocations, each of them beginning with: "In the Name of Allah, who [Bismi'llahi'lladhi]"..................................63

Concerning the ritual prayer of the spiritual elite [salat al-khassa]..71

Concerning the necessity to be constantly on guard against hypocritical display [riya'], the desire to impress one's fellow creatures [ru'yat al-khalq], and vain conceit ['ujb]...............81

AUTHOR'S PROLOGUE

Praise be to Allah for His gracious favour, and blessings and peace be upon the Prince of His Prophets and upon his family and his friends.

The following are the words of our Supreme Helper [Ghawthuna'l-A'zam], the Mainstay of the Arabs and the non-Arabs [Sanad al-'Arab wa'l-'Ajam], the Light of Mankind and the Jinn [Nur ath-Thaqalain], the Axis of East and West [Qutb al-Khafiqain], the Reviver of the Prophetic Example [Muhyi's-Sunna], Abu Muhammad 'Abd al-Qadir al-Hasani al-Husaini al-Jilani (may Allah the Exalted sanctify his innermost being, and may He pour His gracious blessings in abundance upon those who follow his lofty example):

Praise be to Allah, for every book must begin with the declaration of His praise, as every speech must start with the mention of His name. The people of bliss will take delight in praising Him [hereafter] in the abode of requital and reward. By His name is every sickness healed, and with it every grief and tribulation is removed. Toward Him hands are raised in earnest entreaty and supplication, in hardship and in ease, in good times and in bad. He is Attentive [Sami'] to all voices, with all their various forms of speech in different languages, and He is Responsive [Mujib] to those who feel the need to appeal [to Him].

Praise be to Him, therefore, for all that is best and finest, and thanks be to Him for all the favours He has bestowed, for all the gifts He has granted, and for the evidence and guidance He has clearly shown. May His blessings be upon His chosen friend [safi] and Messenger [Rasul], Muhammad, through whom He has guided us out of error, and on his family, his companions, his brother Envoys [Mursalun] and the angels brought near [mala'ika muqarrabun], and may He grant them peace.

Now to address the subject of the present work: One of my friends had been pressing me, urging me in very emphatic terms to compose this book, because of his excellent appreciation of what is right and proper. Of course, Allah is the One who protects from harm ['Asim] in words and deeds, the One who has insight [Muttali'] into consciences [dama'ir] and intentions [niyyat], and the Benefactor [Mun'im] who graciously condescends to facilitate whatever He wishes. Refuge with Him (Almighty and Glorious is He) must be sought through cleansing hearts of pretence [riya'] and hypocrisy [nifaq], and replacing bad deeds with good. He is Forgiving [Ghafir] of sins and mistakes, and Accepting [Qabil] of repentance from His servants.

I came to recognize the sincerity of his [my friend's] wish to acquire real knowledge [ma'rifa] of modes of behaviour consistent with the sacred law [adab shar'iyya], namely obligatory religious duties [fara'id], recommended practices [sunan] and formal refinements [hai'at]; real knowledge of the Maker [Sani'] (Almighty and Glorious is He) through signs [ayat] and indications ['alamat]; then instruction in the Qur'an and Prophetic utterances [alfaz nabawiyya], in discourses [majalis] we shall mention later; and real knowledge of the morals and ethics of the righteous [salihun], which we shall review in the course of the book, so that it may serve as a helper to him in following the path of Allah (Almighty and Glorious is He), in carrying out His commandments and observing His prohibitions.

I found that he had a sincere intention [niyya sadiqa], which I experienced within me among the revelations of the Unseen [futuh al-ghaib], so I gave him a positive response in this matter.

Promptly and eagerly, counting on the reward, hoping for salvation on the Day of Reckoning, I set about the work of compiling this book, with the helpful guidance of the Lord of lords [Rabb al-arbab], the Inspirer of what is right [Mulhim as-sawab], and I have given it the title:

Sufficient Provision for Seekers of the Path of Truth [Al-Ghunya li-Talibi Tariq al-Haqq].

AL-GHUNYA LI-TALIBI TARIQ AL-HAQQ - 1 CONCERNING KNOWLEDGE OF THE CREATOR [SANI'] (ALMIGHTY AND GLORIOUS IS HE)

We shall now give a concise account of our knowledge [ma'rifa] of the Creator [Sani'] (Almighty and Glorious is He), citing the relevant Qur'anic verses [ayat] and evidence from other sources.

The believer must acknowledge and be thoroughly convinced that He is Single [Wahid], Unique [Fard], Eternal [Samad].

Say: "He is Allah, the One! Allah, the Everlasting! He does not beget, nor was He begotten; and there is none comparable unto Him." (112:1-4)

There is nothing like unto Him, and He is the All-Hearing, the All-Seeing. (42:11)

He has no match [shabih] and no counterpart [nazir], no assistant ['awn] and no partner [sharik], no aide [zahir] and no minister [wazir], no peer [nidd] and no adviser [mushir]. He is not a physical body [jism], for if He were, He could be touched. He is not a material substance [jawhar], for if He were, He would be accessible to sensory perception. He is not an accidental property ['arad], for if He were, His existence would be impermanent. He is not an entity with a composite structure [tarkib], nor is He an apparatus [ala] and a combination of elements [ta'lif], a constitution [mahiyya] and a formal definition [tahdid].

It is He, Allah, who is holding the sky aloft and keeping the earth in place, not some property of nature [tabi'a mina't-taba'i'], not some astronomical configuration [tali' mina't-tawali'], not a darkness that looms, and not a light that gleams. He is:

* Hadir. Present to all things through cognition ['ilm]
* Shahid. Witness to all things without physical contact
* 'Aziz. Almighty
* Qahir. Irresistible
* Hakim. Governing
* Qadir. Omnipotent
* Rahim. Merciful
* Ghafir. Forgiver of sins
* Satir. Veiler of faults
* Mu'izz. Ennobling
* Nasir. Supportive
* Ra'uf. Kind
* Khaliq. Creator
* Fatir. Maker
* Awwal. First
* Akhir. Last
* Zahir. Outwardly Manifest
* Batin. Inwardly Concealed
* Fard Ma'bud. Uniquely Worthy of Worship
* Hayyun la yamut. Living, never to die
* Azaliyyun la yafut. Existing from All Eternity, never to pass away
* Abadiyyu'l-Malakut. Eternal Ruler of the Kingdom
* Sarmadiyyu'l-Jabarut. Everlasting Lord of the Dominion
* Qayyumun la yanam. Self-Sustaining, without ever taking rest
* 'Azizun la yudam. Almighty, never to suffer any harm
* Mani'un la yuram. Impregnable, never to be overcome.

Thus to Him belong the Splendid Names [al-Asma' al-'Izam] and all the Noble Talents [al-Mawahib al-Kiram]. He has decreed that all human beings [anam] shall enjoy but a fleeting existence, for He has said:

Everyone who dwells upon the earth must pass away, yet the Face of your Lord still abides, in Majesty and Glory. (55:26,27)

On high is He established, upon the heavenly Throne ['Arsh], encompassing the kingdom [of heaven and earth], while His cognitive awareness ['ilm] embraces all things.

Unto Him good words ascend, and the righteous deed He does exalt. (35:10)

He directs the business [of His entire creation] from the heaven to the earth, then it goes up to Him in one day, the measure of which is a thousand years by your reckoning. (32:5)

He has created all creatures [khala'iq] and their doings [af 'al], and He has predetermined their means of sustenance [arzaq] and their spans of life [ajal]. No one can bring forward what He has postponed, and no one can postpone what He has brought forward.

He willed the whole universe ['alam] and what His creatures would be doing. If He had chosen to prevent them from sinning, they would never have offended against Him. If He had wished them to obey Him entirely, they would certainly have obeyed Him.

He knows the secret and [what is yet] more deeply hidden. (20:7)

He is Cognizant ['Alim] of what is in the breasts [of men]. How should He not know, He who created? And He is the Subtle One [Latif], the All-Aware [Khabir]. (67:14)

He is the One who sets things in motion [Muharrik] and the One who brings things to rest [Musakkin].

No concept of Him can be formed by any stretch of the imagination, nor can He be assessed by any effort of the mind.

He cannot be judged by comparison with human beings. He is far above being likened to that which He has wrought, or being correlated with what He has invented and devised.

He is the Enumerator of breaths [Muhsi'l-anfas], the One 'who reckons with every soul [nafs] according to what it has earned.'

He has indeed counted them, and He has numbered them exactly. And every one of them shall come to Him on the Day of Resurrection, all alone. (19:94,95)

The Hour is surely coming, but I would rather keep it hidden, so that every soul may be recompensed for what it is striving to achieve. (20:15)

So He may reward those who do evil with what they have done, and so He may reward those who do good with goodness. (53:31)

He is Independent of His creation [Ghaniyyun 'an khalqihi], Provident to His creatures [Raziqun li-bariyyatihi]. He supplies food, but He does not need to be fed. He provides sustenance, but He does not need to be sustained. He offers protection, but He does not need to be protected. Every created being [khaliqa] is dependent on Him for all its needs. He created them not for the sake of obtaining some benefit, not to ward off some injury, not because of some motive that prompted Him to do it, and not because of some notion [khatir] that occurred to Him or some idea [fikr] that suggested itself, but by sheer Will [irada mujarrada]. As He Himself has said-and He is the Most Truthful of speakers [Asdaqu'l-qa'ilin]–He is:

Lord of the Throne, the All-Glorious, Doer of what He will. (85:15,16)

He is Uniquely Capable of inventing material substances, of doing away with damage and distress, of transforming substances and altering conditions.

Every day He is about some awesome business [kulla yawmin Huwa fi sha'n]. (55:29)

In other words, He is about the business of steering that which He has predestined [qaddara] toward that which He has scheduled in time [waqqata].

[The believer must also acknowledge and be thoroughly convinced] that He (Exalted is He) is Living in the sense of having life [Hayyun bi-hayat], Knowing in the sense of having knowledge ['Alimun bi-'ilm], Powerful in the sense of having power [Qadirun bi-qudra], Willing in the sense of having will [Muridun bi-irada], Hearing in the sense of having a faculty of hearing [Sami'un bi-sam'], Seeing in the sense of having a faculty of sight [Basirun bi-basar], Consciously Aware in the sense of having conscious awareness [Mudrikun bi-idrak], Articulate in the sense of having a faculty of speech [Mutakallimun bi-kalam], Commanding in the sense of giving orders [Amirun bi-amr], Forbidding in the sense of issuing prohibitions [Nahiyun bi-nahy], and Communicative in the sense of imparting information [Mukhbirun bi-khabar].

[The believer must be convinced] that He (Exalted is He) is Equitable ['Adil] in His ruling and His judgment, and Graciously Beneficent [Muhsin Mutafaddil] in His gifts and His favours; that He is an Originator [Mubdi'] and a Restorer [Mu'id], a Giver of Life [Muhyin] and a Causer of Death [Mumit], a Producer [Muhdith] and an Inventor [Mujid], a Rewarder [Muthib] and a Punisher [Mu'aqib], One who is so Generous [Jawad] that He is never stingy, so Long-suffering [Halim] that He is never in a hurry, so Heedful [Hafiz] that He is never forgetful, so Vigilant [Yaqzan] that He is never inattentive, so Wakeful [Ariq] that He is never negligent.

He causes feelings of constriction [yaqbid] and He causes feelings of expansion [yabsut]. He makes us laugh and He makes us happy. He loves and He hates. He disapproves and He approves. He displays anger and He manifests displeasure. He shows compassion and He forgives. He gives and He withholds. He has two hands [yadan], and each of His two hands is a right hand [yamin].

As He has said (Glorified and Exalted is He):

And the heavens are rolled up in His right hand. (39:67)

According to a report transmitted on the authority of Nafi', Ibn 'Umar (may Allah be well pleased with him and with his father) once said: "Allah's Messenger (Allah bless him and give him peace) was in the pulpit [minbar] when he recited the words of the Qur'an: 'And the heavens are rolled up in His right hand,' then added: 'There they are in His right hand, so He tosses them about, just as a young boy might toss a ball. Then He says: "I am the Almighty! [Ana'l-'Aziz]."'"

Ibn 'Umar went on to say: "I noticed that Allah's Messenger (Allah bless him and give him peace) was quaking up there in the pulpit, so much so that he was on the verge of falling down."

Ibn 'Abbas (may Allah be well pleased with him and with his father) once said: "He clutches all the earths and all the heavens together, yet not even the very edges of them can be seen to protrude from His grasp."

We have it on the authority of Anas ibn Malik, who heard the report from Ibn 'Abbas (may Allah be well pleased with them), that the Prophet (Allah bless him and give him peace) once said:

Those who act justly and fairly [muqsitun] will be mounted, on the Day of Resurrection, in pulpits of light upon the right hand of the All-Merciful [ar-Rahman]-and each of His two hands is a right hand.

He created Adam (peace be upon him) in the form proper to him ['ala suratih]. He planted the Garden of Eden [jannat 'Adn] with His own hand, and the Tree of Bliss [shajarat Tuba] with His own hand. He wrote the Torah with His own hand, and He delivered it to Moses from His hand to his hand. He also spoke to Moses by addressing him directly, with no intermediary channel and without an interpreter.

The hearts [qulub] of His servants are between two fingers of the All-Merciful [ar-Rahman], so He spins them around [yuqallibuha] as He wills, and He instils in them whatever He wishes.

On the Day of Resurrection, the heavens and the earth will be in the palm of His hand, as we know from the tradition [hadith], and He will set His foot in Hell [Jahannam], one part of which will shrink away toward another, while it cries: "Enough! No more!" A group of human beings will issue forth thereafter.

The people of the Garden [of Paradise] will actually see His face, and they will behold it without suffering any injury or harm in the process of beholding it.

As we have learned from the tradition:

He will reveal Himself [yatajalla] to them, and He will give them what they most desire.

He has told us (how Glorious is He as One who tells!):

To those who do good belongs the finest-and an extra reward! [li'lladhina ahsanu'l-husna wa ziyada]. (10:26)

There are those who maintain that 'the finest' refers to the Garden [of Paradise], and that the 'extra reward' is the contemplation of His noble countenance. He has also said (Exalted is He):

That day will faces be resplendent, looking toward their Lord. (75:22,23)

His servants will all be paraded before Him on the Day of Judgment and Doom [yawm al-fasl wa'd-din]. He will take it upon Himself to settle their accounts, and He will not make anyone other than Himself responsible for carrying out this task.

Allah (Exalted is He) created seven heavens, one above another, and seven earths, one below another. [The time it takes to travel] from the highest earth to the lowest heaven is five hundred years, and the distance between each heaven and the next is also a journey of five hundred years. There is water above the seventh heaven, and the Throne of the All-Merciful One ['Arsh ar-Rahman] is above the water. Allah (Exalted is He) is upon the Throne, and beneath Him there are seventy thousand veils of light, of darkness, and of what else He knows best.

The Throne has bearers [hamala] who carry it. As Allah (Almighty and Glorious is He) has said:

Those who bear the Throne, and those who are around it, proclaim the praise of their Lord and believe in Him, and they ask forgiveness for those who believe, [saying]: "Our Lord, You embrace all things in mercy and knowledge; therefore forgive those who repent and follow Your way. Ward off from them the punishment of Hell!" (40:7)

The Throne has a border [hadd], which only Allah knows. [In His own words (Almighty and Glorious is He):]

And you shall see the angels circling around the Throne. (39:75)169

It consists of a single ruby [yaquta hamra'], and its size is equal to that of all the heavens and all the earths combined. Next to the Throne, the Footstool [kursi] is like a ring thrown on the ground in a desert tract.

He (Almighty and Glorious is He) knows what is in the seven heavens and what is between them and what is beneath them, and what is in all the earths and what is beneath them and what is between them, and what is beneath the surface of the land, and what is in the depths of the oceans, and the point of growth of every hair and every tree and every seed that grows, and the place where every leaf will fall, and the number of all of these, and the number of all the pebbles and all the grains of sand and all the specks of dust, and the weights of all the mountains, and the measures of all the oceans, and the actions of His servants and their secret thoughts and the breaths they breathe and the words they speak. He knows everything. Nothing of this is hidden from Him.

He is far above any resemblance to His creation. No place is beyond the scope of His cognizance ['ilm]. It is not permissible, however, to describe Him as being in every place. The correct statement to make is that He is in Heaven [fi's-sama'] upon the Throne ['ala'l-'arsh]. As He Himself has said (let us extol Him as befits His Majesty!):

The All-Merciful has established Himself upon the Throne [ar-Rahmanu 'ala'l-'arshi'stawa]. (20:5)

...then established Himself upon the Throne, the All-Merciful....... [thumma'stawa 'ala'l-'arshi'r-Rahmanu...]. (25:59)

He has also said (Exalted is He):

Unto Him good works ascend, and the righteous deed He does exalt. (35:10)

As for the Prophet (Allah bless him and give him peace), he judged that the Community [Umma] had truly accepted Islam when he said to its members: "Where is Allah?" and they all pointed toward heaven.

The Prophet (Allah bless him and give him peace) once said, according to the tradition [hadith] of Abu Huraira (may Allah be well pleased with him):

When Allah created the creation, He recorded a writ incumbent upon Himself [kataba kitaban 'ala Nafsihi], which is there in His presence above the Throne, [and in it He declared]: "My mercy has overwhelmed My wrath [inna rahmati ghalabat 'ala ghadabi]."

It is proper to use the expression 'firmly established Himself' in a quite straightforward, literal sense [itlaq], without subjecting it to forced interpretation [ta'wil]. It must also be clearly understood to mean the Self-establishment of the Divine Essence [istiwa' adh-Dhat] upon the Throne, not in the sense of bodily sitting down [qu'ud] and making physical contact [mumassa], as maintained by the [heretical sects known as] the Mujassima and the Karramiyya, not in the abstract sense of exaltedness ['uluww] and elevated dignity [rif'a], as maintained by the Ash'ariyya, and not in the sense of control [istila'] and domination [ghalaba], as maintained by the Mu'tazila. These doctrines are unacceptable because they are not in accordance with the sacred law [shar'], and nothing to support them has been handed down to us on the authority of any of the Companions [sahaba] and Successors [tabi'un], the masters of tradition [ashab al-hadith] among our righteous predecessors [as-salaf as-salih]. On the contrary, all the evidence that has been transmitted from them supports the case for the straight forward, literal expression [itlaq].

On the subject of the words of Allah (Almighty and Glorious is He): "The All-Merciful has established Himself on the Throne [ar-Rahmanu 'ala'l-'arshi'stawa]," Umm Salama, the wife of the Prophet (Allah bless him and give him peace), is reported as having transmitted the saying:

Exactly how–that cannot be grasped by the human mind [al-kaif ghair ma'qul]. But that He has 'established Himself' is not beyond our ken [wa'l-istiwa' ghair majhul], so the affirmation of the fact is obligatory, and the negation of it amounts to unbelief [kufr].

In his Sahih [collection of authentic traditions], Muslim ibn al-Hajjaj has traced the transmission of this saying from her, as his authority for attributing it to [her husband] the Prophet (Allah bless him and give him peace). A similar version occurs in the tradition [hadith] of Anas ibn Malik (may Allah be well pleased with him).

Ahmad ibn Hanbal (may Allah bestow His mercy upon him) said, shortly before his death: "The traditional reports [akhbar] concerning the attributes [sifat] [of Allah] must simply be accepted as they have been handed down to us, without [erring in one direction by] giving them an anthropomorphic interpretation [tashbih], and without [erring in the other direction by] negating the very existence of those attributes [ta'til].

He also said, according to the account of his teaching transmitted by some of his followers: "I am not a professor of theology [sahib kalam], and I do not see any value in making theological pronouncements on any of these subjects, except for what is stated in the Book of Allah (Almighty and Glorious is He), or in a tradition [hadith] that has been handed down from the Prophet himself (Allah bless him and give him peace), or from his Companions [ashab] (may Allah be well pleased with them all), or from the Successors [tabi'un]. As far as anything other than this is concerned, theological debate on the subject is not to be commended. The attributes of the Lord (Almighty and Glorious is He) should therefore not be spoken about in terms of how and why. The only people who speak in such terms are the doubting sceptics [shukkak]."

It was on a different occasion, according to another account of his teaching, that Ahmad [ibn Hanbal] (may Allah bestow His mercy upon him) said: "We believe that Allah (Almighty and Glorious is He) is upon the Throne, however He wills [kaifa sha'a] and just as He wills [kama sha'a], without reference to any definition or description that might be offered by someone attempting to describe or define."

[We believe this] because of what has been reported to us on the authority of Sa'id ibn al-Musayyib, to the effect that Ka'b al-Ahbar once said: "Allah (Exalted is He) has said in the Torah:

I, Allah, am above My servants, and My Throne is above the whole of My creation, and I am upon My Throne, whereon I regulate [the affairs of] My servants, and nothing pertaining to My servants is ever hidden from Me."

Indeed, the fact that He (Almighty and Glorious is He) is upon the Throne is mentioned in every Scripture that has been revealed [fi kulli kitabin unzila] to every Prophet who has been sent forth to deliver His message ['ala kulli nabiyyin ursila], without further explanation [bi-la kaif].

In all the records that are still available to us, Allah (Exalted is He) is also characterized as possessing the attributes of Exaltedness ['uluww] and Omnipotence [qudra], as exercising control [istila'] and domination [ghalaba] over the whole of His creation from the Throne, and so on.

None of this, therefore, can be what is meant by His 'Self-establishment' [istiwa']. Self-establishment must be one of the attributes of the Divine Essence [sifat adh-Dhat], since He has informed us of it, mentioned it explicitly, and stated it emphatically in seven verses [ayat] of His Book, and since this view is confirmed by the Prophetic tradition [sunna ma'thura]. It must be an attribute [sifa] that is intrinsic to Him [lazima lahu] and properly befitting Him [la'iqa bihi], like the Hand [yad], the Face [wajh], the Eye ['ain], the Hearing [sam'], the Sight [basar], the Life [hayat] and the Power [qudra], all of which are properly attributed to Him, as well as His being Creator [Khaliq], Sustainer [Raziq], Giver of Life [Muhyin] and Causer of Death [Mumit].

We do not depart from the Book and the Sunna. We read the Qur'anic verse [aya] and the traditional report [khabar]. We believe what these two sources contain, and we entrust the detailed understanding [kaifiyya] of the [divine] attributes to the knowledge ['ilm] of Allah (Almighty and Glorious is He). As Sufyan ibn 'Uyaina (may Allah bestow His mercy upon him) once put it: "Just as Allah (Exalted is He) has described Himself in His Book." In other words, the reading of it is self-explanatory, and there is no need of further interpretative commentary [tafsir]. This is all that is required of us, because the rest is a mystery [ghaib], the comprehension of which is beyond the scope of the human mind ['aql].

We beg Allah (Exalted is He) to grant pardon ['afw] and well-being ['afiya], and we take refuge with Him in case we should say anything about Him or His attributes that we have not been taught by Him or by His Messenger (Allah bless him and give him peace).

[The believer must also acknowledge and be thoroughly convinced] that He (Exalted is He) descends each night to the heaven of this lower world [sama' ad-dunya], however He wills and just as He wills, and that He then forgives those who have sinned, erred, offended and disobeyed; those of His servants, that is to say, whom He chooses and wishes to forgive. Hallowed and Exalted is the All-High, the Most High [tabaraka wa ta'ala'l-'Aliyyu'l-A'la].

There is no god but He [la ilaha illa Hu]. His are the Most Beautiful Names [lahu'l-asma'u'l-husna]. (20:8)

This is not to be understood as meaning the descent of [Allah's] mercy [nuzul ar-rahma] and His spiritual reward [thawab], as maintained by the Mu'tazila and the Ash'ariyya, because we know from the report transmitted by 'Ubada ibn as-Samit (may Allah be well pleased with him) that Allah's Messenger (Allah bless him and give him peace) once said:

Allah (Hallowed and Exalted is He) descends each night to the heaven of this lower world, when the last third of the night is still remaining, and He says: "Is there anyone begging?" --so that He may grant him his request. "Is there anyone seeking forgiveness?" --so that He may forgive him. "Is there anyone held captive ['anin]?"--so that He may release him from his captivity. [This continues] until it is time for the dawn prayer to be performed, then our Lord (Hallowed and Exalted is He) ascends on high.

According to another traditional report [riwaya], also on the authority of 'Ubada ibn as-Samit (may Allah be well pleased with him), the Prophet (Allah bless him and give him peace) said:

Allah (Hallowed and Exalted is He) descends each night to the heaven of this lower world, when the last third of the night is still remaining, and He says: "Is there not one of My servants who will call upon Me, so that I may respond to him? Is there not someone, a person who has wronged himself [zalim li-nafsih], who will call upon Me, so that I may forgive him? Is there not someone, a person who lacks the sustenance he needs, who will call upon Me, so that I may procure his sustenance for him? Is there not some victim of oppression [mazlum], who will invoke My name, so that I may help him? Is there not someone held in captivity, who will call upon Me, so that I may release him?" He goes on like this until the dawn appears, and then He ascends to His Pedestal [kursi].

This same tradition [hadith] has been transmitted, with some differences in the wording, on the authority of Abu Huraira, Jabir and 'Ali (may Allah be well pleased with them all). Versions of it have also been handed down from 'Abdu'llah ibn Mas'ud, Abu'd-Darda', Ibn 'Abbas and 'A'isha (may the good pleasure of Allah be upon them), all of whom attribute the saying to Allah's Messenger (Allah bless him and give him peace). This explains why they used to regard it as preferable to perform the ritual prayer [salat] in the last part of the night, rather than in the first part of it.

As reported by Abu Bakr, the Champion of Truth [as-Siddiq] (may Allah be well pleased with him), the Prophet (Allah bless him and give him peace) also said:

Allah (Almighty and Glorious is He) descends to the heaven of this lower world on the night of the middle of Sha'ban, and He then forgives every soul, excepting only the individual in whose heart there is malice [shahna'], or the attribution of partners [shirk] to Allah (Almighty and Glorious is He).

Abu Huraira (may Allah be well pleased with him) is reported as having said that he once heard Allah's Messenger (Allah bless him and give him peace) say:

When the first half of the night has elapsed, Allah (Almighty and Glorious is He) descends to the heaven of this lower world, and then He says: "Is there anyone seeking forgiveness, that I may forgive him? Is there anyone begging, that I may give to him? Is there anyone repenting, that I may relent toward him?" [This continues] until the early dawn [fajr] begins to break.

Somebody once said to Ishaq ibn Rahawaih: "What are these traditions [ahadith] you are relating, to the effect that Allah (Exalted is He) descends to the lowest heaven? Does Allah then rise up again? Does He move about?" Ishaq replied by asking the questioner: "Would you say of Allah (Exalted is He) that it is possible for Allah to descend and to ascend, and to do so without moving about?" When the man gave the answer "Yes," Ishaq went on to ask: "So why do you have a problem with this?"

Yahya ibn Mu'in once said: "If a Jahmi asks you: 'How does He descend?' you should reply by asking: 'How did He ascend?'" As for al-Fudail ibn 'Iyad (may Allah bestow His mercy upon him), he offered this advice: "If a Jahmi tells you: 'I am a disbeliever [kafir] in a Lord who is supposed to descend,' you should say to him: 'I am a believer [mu'min] in a Lord who does whatever He wills.'"

When somebody once told Shuraik ibn 'Abdi'llah (may Allah bestow His mercy upon him): "We have here a group of people who refuse to accept these traditions [ahadith]," he is said to have replied: "Has anyone handed down to us [reports transmitted by] names that cannot be traced back to Allah's Messenger (Allah bless him and give him peace)? [It is from these traditions that we have learned the rules of] the ritual prayer [salat], the fast [siyam], the alms-due [zakat] and the pilgrimage [hajj], and through these traditions we have acquired knowledge ['arafna] of Allah (Almighty and Glorious is He)."

AL-GHUNYA LI-TALIBI TARIQ AL-HAQQ - 2
CONCERNING CONTENTMENT [RIDA].

As for contentment [rida], the fundamental guidance on the subject is contained in the words of Allah (Almighty and Glorious is He):

Allah is well pleased with them, and they are well pleased with Him. (58:22)

--and in His words (Blessed and Exalted is He):

Their Lord gives them good news of mercy from Him, and good pleasure, and Gardens [of Paradise] in which they shall have lasting bliss. (9:21)

Furthermore, according to a traditional report, transmitted on the authority of Ibn 'Abbas (may Allah be well pleased with him and with his father), Allah's Messenger (Allah bless him and give him peace) once said:

The full flavour of true faith [iman] is tasted by one who is content with Allah (Almighty and Glorious is He) as a Lord [Rabb].

[The Caliph] 'Umar ibn al-Khattab once wrote to Abu Musa al-Ash'ari (may Allah be well pleased with them both):

"The point I wish to emphasize is this: All goodness resides in contentment [rida], so if you are capable of being content, [well and good]. If not, you must be patient [fa-'sbir]."

It was Qatada (may Allah the Exalted bestow His mercy upon him) who said, in commenting on the words of Allah (Almighty and Glorious is He):

And if one of them receives tidings of the birth of a female, his face remains darkened, and he is inwardly furious. (16:58)

--"This describes the attitude of those Arabs who attribute partners to Allah [mushriki'l-'Arab]. Allah (Almighty and Glorious is He) has thus informed us of the badness of their attitude. As for the believer [mu'min], he is worthily disposed to be content with whatever Allah (Exalted is He) has allotted to him."

The judgment of Allah (Almighty and Glorious is He) is better than a man's judgment on his own behalf. That which Allah has decreed for you concerning something you dislike, O son of Adam, may be even better for you than that which Allah has decreed for you concerning something you like. You must therefore observe your duty to Allah (Exalted is He), and be content to accept His decision.

Allah (Blessed and Exalted is He) has told us:

But it may happen that you hate a thing that is good for you, and it may happen that you love a thing which is bad for you. Allah knows, and you know not. (2:216)

That is to say, [He knows, and you do not know] what is in the best interest of your religion [din] and your worldly life, for Allah (Almighty and Glorious is He) has kept concealed from His creatures the things that are to their advantage. He has charged them with servitude ['ubudiyya] to Him, by requiring fulfilment of the commandments and observance of the prohibitions [of the Sacred Law], submissive resignation to that which is foreordained [maqdur], and contentment [rida] with the divine decree [qada'] in every respect, whether it be in their favour or to their disadvantage. He has appropriated the consequences and the benefits unto Himself exclusively

(Almighty and Glorious is He). It is therefore necessary for the servant to be constantly engaged in worshipful obedience to his Master [Mawla], to be content with whatever Allah has allotted to him, and to harbour no doubts about Him.

As you should also be well aware, the amount of trouble experienced by any individual creature is in proportion to his quarrel with destiny [qadar] over that which is foreordained [maqdur], his compliance with his own desire [hawa'], and his lack of contentment [rida] with the divine decree [qada']. Whenever someone is content to accept the divine decree, that person can enjoy rest and relaxation. Whenever someone is not content with it, on the other hand, his experience of misery and trouble can only be prolonged, and he will still obtain nothing from this world except that which has been allotted to him. As long as his personal desire persists in making its demands upon him, he cannot be content to accept the divine decree, because that desire is in contention with the Lord of Truth (Almighty and Glorious is He), and so his troubles can only intensify and multiply.

The procurement of ease and comfort is the result of opposition to personal desire [hawa'], because it is bound to involve contentment [rida] with the divine decree [qada']. The procurement of trouble and discomfort, on the other hand, is the result of compliance with personal desire, because it is bound to involve contention with the Lord of Truth (Almighty and Glorious is He). So may desire not be there, and if it is, let us not be!

Should contentment [rida] be classed as one of the spiritual states [ahwal], or as one of the spiritual stations [maqamat]? On this point there are differences of opinion among the qualified scholars and experts in the spiritual path [tariqa].

According to the people of 'Iraq, it is one of the spiritual states [ahwal]. It is not subject, they maintain, to active acquisition [kasb] by the servant [of the Lord]. It is rather an occurrence or visitation [nazila], a condition that settles for a while within the inner feeling, like all the other spiritual states [ahwal], then changes and passes away, as another state arrives to take its place.

According to the Khurasanis, on the other hand, contentment [rida] is one of the spiritual stations [maqamat]. They consider it to be the final stage of absolute trust in the Lord [tawakkul], so that it represents the ultimate degree to which the servant [of the Lord] can attain through his own acquisitive capacity [iktisab].

It is possible to reconcile these two views, by stating the case as follows:

The initial stage of contentment [bidayat ar-rida] is subject to active acquisition [muktasaba] by the servant [of the Lord], which means that it is one of the spiritual stations [maqamat]. But its final stage [nihaya] is one of the spiritual states [ahwal], which means that it is not subject to active acquisition.

In simple terms, someone who is content [radi] is someone who does not object to the foreordainment [taqdir] of Allah (Almighty and Glorious is He).

It was Abu 'Ali ad-Daqqaq (may Allah the Exalted bestow His mercy upon him) who said:

"Contentment [rida] does not mean that you are not affected by the experience of trial and tribulation. Contentment [rida] simply means that you do not object to the divine decision [hukm] and decree [qada']."

The wise elders [mashayikh] (may Allah the Exalted bestow His mercy upon them) have often said:

"Contentment with the divine decree [ar-rida bi'l-qada'] is Allah's most splendid gateway, and it is this world's Garden of Paradise. That is to say, when someone is blessed with the honour of contentment [rida], he has already received the most abundant welcome, and has been honoured with the most exalted nearness."

It is said that a pupil [tilmidh] once asked his teacher [ustadh]: "Is the servant aware that Allah (Blessed and Exalted is He) is well pleased with him?" "No," replied the teacher, "how can he know that, when His good pleasure [rida] is imperceptible?" But the pupil said: "Oh yes, he does recognize it," so the teacher asked: "How?" The pupil then explained: "When I find that my inner feeling is well pleased with Allah (Exalted is He), I know that He is well pleased with me." So the teacher said: "You have done very well, young man!"

It is indeed true that the servant will not be well pleased with Allah, unless the Lord of Truth (Glorious is His Majesty) is well pleased with him. Allah (Almighty and Glorious is He) has told us:

Allah is well pleased with them, and they are well pleased with Him. (58:22)

--That is to say, because of His good pleasure [rida] with them, they are well pleased with Him.

It is said that Moses [Musa] (peace be upon him) once had a request to make of his Lord (Almighty and Glorious is He), so he said: "My God [Ilahi], point out to me a deed, such that, if I perform it, You will be well pleased with me." The Lord said:

"You are not capable of that," so Moses (peace be upon him) sank to the ground, prostrating himself [sajid] in humble submission. Allah (Almighty and Glorious is He) then conveyed to him by way of inspiration [awha ilai-hi]: "O son of 'Imran, My good pleasure resides in your contentment with My decree [inna rida'i fi rida-ka bi-qada'i]."

Let us also consider the following wise sayings:

"If a person wishes to arrive at the stage of contentment [rida], let him stick to the course upon which Allah (Almighty and Glorious is He) has conferred His good pleasure [rida]."

"Contentment [rida] is of two kinds, namely: (1) ready approval of Him [rida bi-hi], and (2) resigned acceptance of Him [rida 'an-hu]. There is ready approval of Him as a Manager [Mudabbir], and there is resigned acceptance of Him with respect to what He decrees as a Ruler [Hakim] and as a Judge [Fasil]."

"When someone is content [radi], it means that even if Hell [Jahannam] were to be placed on his right side, he would not ask for it to be moved over to his left side."

"Contentment [rida] means the expulsion of disagreeable feelings from the heart, so that nothing remains except happiness and joy."

Rabi'a al-'Adawiyya (may Allah the Exalted bestow His mercy upon her) was once asked the question: "When is the servant [of the Lord] content [radi] with the divine decree [bi-'l-qada']?" To this she replied (may Allah the Exalted bestow His mercy upon her): "When he is happy with affliction, just as he is happy with gracious favour."

It is said that ash-Shibli (may Allah the Exalted bestow His mercy upon him) once uttered the expression:

There is neither any power nor any strength except with Allah. [la hawla wa la quwwata illa bi'llah.]

--in the presence of al-Junaid (may Allah the Exalted bestow His mercy upon him), so al-Junaid (may Allah bestow His mercy upon him) told him: "In saying that, you are prompted by a feeling of annoyance, and the feeling of annoyance is due to the lack of contentment [rida] with the divine decree [qada']."

It was Abu Sulaiman [ad-Darani] (may Allah the Exalted bestow His mercy upon him) who said:

"Contentment [rida] means that you do not ask Allah to grant you the Garden of Paradise, and that you do not appeal to Him for refuge from the Fire of Hell."

Dhu 'n-Nun al-Misri (may Allah the Exalted bestow His mercy upon him) once said:

"These are three of the symptoms of contentment [rida]: (1) the lack of personal preference in advance of the divine decree [qada'], (2) the absence of bitterness in the wake of the divine decree, and (3) the arousal of love in the midst of trial and tribulation."

He also said (may Allah the Exalted bestow His mercy upon him):

"It is the happiness of the heart with the bitterness of the divine decree [qada']."

When Abu 'Uthman [al-Hiri] (may Allah the Exalted bestow His mercy upon him) was asked to explain the saying of the Prophet (Allah bless him and give him peace):

What I ask of you is contentment [rida] in the wake of the divine decree [qada'].

--he said: "That is because contentment [rida] in advance of the divine decree [qada'] is only the prior determination to be content, while contentment [rida] in the wake of the divine decree [qada'] is the actual experience of contentment [huwa'r-rida]."

As we learn from a traditional report, someone once told al-Husain ibn 'Ali ibn Abi Talib (may Allah be well pleased with him and with his father) that Abu Dharr (may Allah be well pleased with him) used to say:

"Poverty is dearer to me than affluence, sickness is dearer to me than health, and death is dearer to me than life."

So he said: "May Allah bestow His mercy upon Abu Dharr. As for myself, I say: 'When somecne relies upon the excellence of Allah's choice, he does not wish for anything other than that which Allah has chosen for him.'"

[Abu 'Ali] al-Fudail ibn 'Iyad once said to Bishr al-Hafi ["the Barefoot"] (may Allah the Exalted bestow His mercy upon them both):

"Contentment [rida] is more meritorious than abstinence [zuhd] from this world, because when someone is content [radi], he does not wish for anything above his actual situation."

The view expressed by al-Fudail is the correct one, because it refers to contentment with one's actual condition [ar-rida bi'l-hal], and all that is good resides in contentment with one's actual condition. Allah (Almighty and Glorious is He) said to Moses [Musa] (peace be upon him):

"O Moses! I have preferred you above mankind by My messages and by My speaking [to you]. So hold that which I have given you, and be among the thankful." (7:144)

That is to say: "Be content with that which I have bestowed upon you. Do not go looking for another situation, and be among the thankful." In other words: "Be content with making the most of your actual condition [hifz al-hal]."

Likewise to our own Prophet Muhammad (Allah bless him and give him peace), He said (Exalted is He):

And strain not your eyes toward that which We have given for some pairs among them to enjoy-- the flower of this world's life, that We may thereby put them to the test. (20:131)

As well as giving this instruction to His Prophet (blessing and peace be upon him), He also commanded him to make the most of his actual condition [hifz al-hal], and to be content with the divine decree and bestowal of provision [ar-rida bi'l-qada' wa'l-'ata'], in His words (Exalted is He):

And the provision of your Lord is better and more lasting. (20:131)

That is to say: "That which We have bestowed upon you--in the way of Prophethood [Nubuwwa], knowledge ['ilm], satisfaction [qana'a], patience [sabr], authority in religion [wilayat ad-din] and the role of exemplar [qudwa] therein--is far superior to that which We have bestowed upon anyone other than you."

All goodness therefore resides in making the most of one's actual condition [hifz al-hal], in being content with it, and in refraining from taking an interest in any condition apart from it, because the only possibilities, as far as that [other condition] is concerned, are the following: (1) it is your own allotted portion [qism], (2) it is the allotted portion [qism] of someone other than yourself, or (3) it is not a portion [qism] allotted to anyone, but something that Allah (Exalted is He) has caused to exist as a temptation [fitna].

If it is indeed your own allotted portion [qism], it is bound to come your way, whether you wish for it or not. It is therefore inappropriate for you to exhibit bad manners and greediness in its pursuit, for that would be judged unworthy by the standard of reason ['aql] and knowledge ['ilm].

If it is the allotted portion [qism] of someone other than yourself, you must not waste your time and energy on that which you cannot obtain, and which will never come your way. If it is not a portion [qism] allotted to anyone, but merely a temptation [fitna], how could any intelligent person be content, and how could any sensible person consider it worthwhile, to seek and attempt to procure a temptation for himself?

Certain experts on the subject have said:

"Contentment [rida] with the divine decree [qada'] means that there is no significant distinction, as far as you are concerned, between what you like and what you dislike about His decree (Almighty and Glorious is He)."

One of them has said:

"It means patience [sabr] in enduring the bitterness of the divine decree [qada']."

Another has said:

"It means laying the palms of one's hands on the ground [i.e., prostrating oneself] in the presence of Allah (Almighty and Glorious is He), and submitting [taslim] to His rulings [ahkam]."

Another has said:

"It means leaving it to the Manager [Mudabbir] to select the best option."

Yet another has said:

"It means giving up personal preference [ikhtiyar]."

One of them has said:

"The people who really experience contentment [ahl ar-rida] are those who eradicate personal preference from their hearts. This means that they accord no special preference to any of the various things they may want for themselves, nor to any of the things by which they intend to please Allah. They make no requests of Him, and they do not try to find out about a ruling [hukm] before it comes down [from Him]. So, when a ruling [hukm] does come down from Allah, in as much as they are not eagerly awaiting it, and have not tried to learn about it in advance, they are content with it and take pleasure and delight in it."

The same person has also said:

"Allah has some servants who see it as a gracious favour, bestowed upon them by Allah, when the sentence [hukm] of trial and tribulation is imposed upon them, so they thank Him for it and accept it gladly. But then they come to realize, in the wake of their delight in gracious favours, that their preoccupation with the benefaction [ni'ma], instead of with the Benefactor [Mun'im], amounts to a shortcoming. Their hearts are now preoccupied with the Benefactor [Mun'im], instead of with the benefaction [ni'ma], and so the affliction runs its course over them, while their hearts are unaffected by it.

Once they have settled into this spiritual station [maqam], and have made it their permanent residence, their Master [Mawla] will transport them to a level that is even loftier for them and more elevated than that, because there is no limit and no end to His gifts (Almighty and Glorious is He)."

At the very least, contentment [rida] must mean that one ceases to yearn for anything apart from Allah (Almighty and Glorious is He), since Allah (Almighty and Glorious is He) has declared it blameworthy to yearn for anything other than Him (Almighty and Glorious is He).

Yahya ibn Kathir is reported as having said: "I read the Torah [Tawrah], and in it I saw that Allah (Glory be to Him and Exalted is He) says:

'Accursed is he whose reliance is placed upon a creature like himself.'"

In one of the traditions [akhbar], it is reported that Allah (Glory be to Him) says:

By My Might, My Majesty, My Generosity and My Glory, I shall cut off with despair the hope of anyone who pins his hope on anything other than Me. I shall cause him to wear the garment of shame among the people. I shall banish him from My proximity, and I shall cut him off from access to Me. Will he go on pinning his hope, in the midst of adversities, on anything other than Me, when adversities are under My control, and I am the Ever-Living [al-Hayy]? Will he go on appealing to others apart from Me? Will he go on knocking with his mind at the doors of others apart from Me, when they are locked and their keys are in My hand?

In another tradition [khabar], it is reported that Allah (Almighty and Glorious is He) says:

Whenever a servant holds fast to Me, rather than to My creation, that fact becomes known from his heart and his intention [niyya], so the heavens and the earth and all within them conspire to bring about his downfall, but I provide him with a means of escape therefrom. And whenever a servant clings to a created entity, rather than to Me, I cut away the cords of heaven from above him, and I turn the earth into a swamp beneath his feet. Then I bring him to ruination in this world, and I make him suffer misery therein.

One of the Companions [Sahaba] (may the good pleasure [ridwan] of Allah the Exalted be upon them all) is reported as having said: "I once heard Allah's Messenger (Allah bless him and give him peace) say:

'If someone takes pride in human beings, he deserves to be treated with contempt.'"

In the words of another wise saying:

"If a person relies upon a creature like himself, he deserves to be treated with contempt. Because of his ambitious desire [tama'] to get whatever he wants, he is prevented from consulting his inner feeling, distracted from his true aspiration, and exposed to degradation and abasement. Two things are therefore stacked against him, namely, humiliation in this world and remoteness from Allah (Almighty and Glorious is He), without the addition of one single atom to increase his sustenance."

One of the experts had this to say:

"I know of nothing more harmful to spiritual aspirants [muridin] and seekers [talibin] than ambitious desire [tama']. I know of nothing more detrimental to their hearts, nothing more likely to make them suffer degradation, nothing more injurious to their inner feelings, nothing more likely to keep them far removed from their goal, and nothing more serious as a distraction from their true aspiration."

"As for why this is so, the reason is simply that it amounts to a form of polytheism [shirk], wherever they may be, because one of them has attributed a partner to Allah (Almighty and Glorious is He), inasmuch as he has focused his ambitious desire [tama'] on a creature like himself, who is powerless to cause any harm or provide any benefit, and incapable of giving or withholding any gift. He has thereby assigned the power of the King [Malik] to His slave [mamluk]. So what of his claim to piety [wara']? His claim to piety will not be recognized as genuine, until he attributes all things to their Owner [Malik] (Almighty and Glorious is He), then seeks to obtain them from Him, and does not seek to obtain them from anyone other than Him."

As someone else has explained:

"Ambitious desire [tama'] has a root and a branch. The root of it is heedless neglect, while its branch consists of hypocritical ostentation [riya'], promoting an undeserved reputation [sum'a], pretence and affectation, and a fondness for acquiring prestige in the eyes of the public."

Jesus ['Isa] (peace be upon him) once said to the Disciples [Hawariyyin]:

"Ambitious desire [tama'] is the deadly enemy of inspiration [wahy]."

One of the experts on this subject is reported as having said:

"It happened one day that I felt a strong desire for something belonging to this world, but then an invisible voice [hatif] called out to me, saying: 'O you there! Since the free man with spiritual aspirations [al-hurr al-murid] can find whatever he seeks in the presence of Allah, it ill befits him to depend in his heart upon servile creatures ['abid]."

You should also know that Allah has certain servants ['ibad] who are unconscious of the fact that ambition must be focused on the one who has the power to grant what they desire, until they receive the blessing of grace [baraka] from an unexpected source. Only then do they realize that the state of ambitious desire [tama'] is a defective condition among the spiritual states [ahwal]. It is a lower degree than all the degrees attained by those, among the people of absolute trust in the Lord, whose knowledge is based on direct experience [al-'arifin min ahl at-tawakkul].

No trace of ambitious desire [tama'] can enter and settle in the heart of the spiritual aspirant [murid], unless it be on account of total remoteness from Allah (Almighty and Glorious is He), due to his having focused his ambition on a creature like himself, and because fear has not deterred him from doing so, even though he is well aware that his Master [Mawla] knows absolutely everything about him.

AL-GHUNYA LI-TALIBI TARIQ AL-HAQQ - 3 CONCERNING ABSOLUTE TRUST IN THE LORD [TAWAKKUL].

As for putting all one's trust in the Lord [tawakkul], the basic guidance on the subject is contained in His words (Almighty and Glorious is He):

And when someone puts all his trust in Allah, He will be enough for him. (65:3)

--and in His words (Exalted is He):

And put all your trust [in Allah], if you are indeed believers. (5:23)

According to a traditional report, transmitted on the authority of 'Abdu'llah ibn Mas'ud (may Allah be well pleased with him), Allah's Messenger (Allah bless him and give him peace) once said:

I saw the religious communities [umam] at the gathering place [mawsim], and I noticed that my Community [Ummati] filled both the plain and the mountainside, so I was astonished at their number and their condition. I was asked: "Are you well pleased?" "Yes," said I. Then I was told: "Together with these, seventy thousand will enter the Garden of Paradise without undergoing any reckoning. They do not play with fire. They do not look for bad omens. They do not practice subterfuge. They put all their trust in their Lord."

On hearing this, 'Ukasha ibn Mihsan al-Asadi stood up and said: "O Messenger of Allah, appeal to Allah that He may include me among them!" So Allah's Messenger (Allah bless him and give him peace) said: "O Allah, let him be included among them!" Then someone else jumped up and said: "Appeal to Allah that He may include me among them!" To this he responded (Allah bless him and give him peace) by saying: "'Ukasha has arrived there ahead of you!"

The real meaning [haqiqa] of absolute trust [tawakkul] is delegating all one's affairs to Allah (Almighty and Glorious is He), making a clean escape from the murky darkness and gloom of personal choice and self-management, and advancing to the arenas where the [divine] decrees [ahkam] and foreordainment [taqdir] are experienced directly.

The servant [of the Lord] must be convinced that there is no possibility of changing the allotment of destiny [qisma], which means that whatever has been allotted to him cannot pass him by, and that he can never obtain what has not been allotted to him. His heart will then become reconciled to this, and he will feel confident in relying on the promise [wa'd] of his Master [Mawla]. He will therefore receive from his Master [Mawla].

Putting one's trust in the Lord [tawakkul] is actually the first of three stages, namely: (1) the basic sense of trust [tawakkul], then (2) the act of surrender or resignation [taslim], and then (3) the act of delegation [tafwid]. The person who is at the stage of basic trust [al-mutawakkil] is one who feels confident in relying on the promise [wa'd] of his Lord. The person who is at the stage of surrender or resignation [sahib at-taslim] is one who is content to rely on His knowledge ['ilm]. The person who is at the stage of delegation [sahib at-tafwid] is one who is happy to accept His judgment [hukm].

There are many wise sayings on this subject, for instance:

"Trust is an initial stage [at-tawakkul bidaya], surrender or resignation is a middle stage [at-taslim wasat], and delegation is a final stage [at-tafwid nihaya]."

"Trust is the attribute of the believers [at-tawakkul sifat al-mu'minin], surrender or resignation is the attribute of the saints [at-taslim sifat al-awliya'], and delegation is the attribute of those who realize and affirm the Divine Oneness [at-tafwid sifat al-muwahhidin]."

"Trust is the attribute of the common folk [at-tawakkul sifat al-'awamm], surrender or resignation is the attribute of the elite [at-taslim sifat al-khawass], and delegation is the attribute of the elite of the elite [at-tafwid sifat khawass al-khawass]."

"Trust is the attribute of the Prophets [at-tawakkul sifat al-Anbiya'], surrender or resignation is the attribute of Abraham [at-taslim sifat Ibrahim], and delegation is the attribute of our own Prophet [Muhammad] [at-tafwid sifat Nabiyyi-na] (may the blessings of Allah be upon them all)."

The point of this last saying is that trust in the Lord [tawakkul], as a complete and perfect reality [haqiqa], was experienced by Abraham, the Bosom Friend of Allah [Ibrahim al-Khalil] (peace be upon him), at the moment when he said to Gabriel [Jabril] (peace be upon him) : "As for recognizing your existence, oh no!" This was because his personal identity [nafs] had vanished without leaving a trace behind, so that he saw nothing together with Allah (Exalted is He), other than Allah (Almighty and Glorious is He).

It was Sahl ibn 'Abdi'llah (may Allah the Exalted bestow His mercy upon him) who said:

"The first stage in absolute trust [tawakkul] is where the position of the servant between the hands of Allah (Almighty and Glorious is He) is just like that of the corpse between the hands of the ritual washer of the dead [ghasil], who turns the body this way and that, as he wishes, while it has no independent movement or control of its actions. Someone who puts all his trust [al-mutawakkil] in Allah (Glory be to Him and Exalted is He) is therefore in a state where he does not ask for anything, does not wish for anything, does not reject anything, and does not hold on to anything."

In the words of another wise saying:

"Trust in the Lord [tawakkul] is letting oneself go [istirsal]."

It was Hamdun [al-Qassar] (may Allah the Exalted bestow His mercy upon him) who said:

"It is holding fast [i'tisam] to Allah (Almighty and Glorious is He)."

Ibrahim al-Khawwas (may Allah the Exalted bestow His mercy upon him) had this to say on the subject:

"The real meaning [haqiqa] of absolute trust in the Lord [tawakkul] is the detachment of fear and hope from everything apart from Allah (Almighty and Glorious is He)."

In the words of another wise saying:

"Absolute trust in the Lord [tawakkul] is living one day at a time, and dispensing with concern about tomorrow."

It was Abu 'Ali ar-Rudhbari (may Allah the Exalted bestow His mercy upon him) who said:

"There are three stages in the development of absolute trust in the Lord [tawakkul], namely: (1) when he is granted a gift, the recipient is grateful, and when he is deprived, he is patient; (2) as far the servant [of the Lord] is concerned, to be deprived and to be granted a gift are one and the same; (3) deprivation combined with gratitude is what he likes best of all, because he is aware that this is Allah's preference (Exalted is He) on his behalf."

Ja'far al-Khuldi is reported as having said: "Ibrahim al-Khawwas (may Allah the Exalted bestow His mercy upon him) once said:

"'As I was travelling along the road to Mecca, I caught sight of a wild-looking figure, so I said to it: 'Are you a jinn' or a human being?' It replied: 'I am a jinn', of course, so I asked: 'Where are you going?' The following conversation then took place between us:

"I am on my way to Mecca," said the jinni.

"What," said I, "with no provision for the journey, and without a camel to ride on?"

"Yes," said the jinni, "among our kind as well, there are those who travel on the basis of absolute trust in the Lord ['ala 't-tawakkul]."

"And what," I asked, "is absolute trust in the Lord [tawakkul]?"

"'It is receiving from Allah," the jinni told me.'"

Sahl [ibn 'Abdi'llah ibn Yunus at-Tustari] (may Allah the Exalted bestow His mercy upon him) once said:

"It is the conscious acknowledgment [ma'rifa] of the Provider of the sustenance of all creatures [Mu'ti arzaqi'l-makhluqin]. No one is genuinely capable of absolute trust in the Lord [tawakkul], until the sky in his sight is like brass, and the earth is like iron, so that rain does not fall from the sky, and plants do not sprout from the earth, yet between these two, he is well aware that Allah will never forget to provide him with the sustenance He has guaranteed to him."

In the words of another wise saying:

"It means that you do not disobey Allah (Exalted is He) on account of your sustenance."

As a certain wise man put it:

"In order to have absolute trust in the Lord [tawakkul], it is sufficient that you seek for yourself no helper other than Allah (Exalted is He), for your sustenance no keeper other than Him, and for your conduct no witness other than Him."

It was al-Junaid (may Allah the Exalted bestow His mercy upon him) who said:

"Absolute trust [tawakkul] means that you devote yourself totally to your Lord, and that you turn your attention away from all those who are beneath him."

In the words of an-Nuri (may Allah the Exalted bestow His mercy upon him):

"It means that you let your self-management become absorbed into His management [tadbir], and that you are perfectly satisfied with Allah as a Trustee [Wakil], as a Manager [Mudabbir] and as a Helper [Nasir]."

Allah Himself (Exalted is He) has told us:

And Allah is sufficient as a Trustee. (4:81)

In the words of another wise saying:

"Absolute trust [tawakkul] is the state in which the humble servant [al-'abd adh-dhalil] is utterly content with the All-Majestic Lord [ar-Rabb al-Jalil], just as the Bosom Friend [al-Khalil] was utterly content with the All-Majestic [al-Jalil], so much so that he took no notice of the attentive presence of Gabriel [Jabril] (peace be upon him)."

To quote yet another wise saying:

"It means abstaining from self-motivated activity, in complete reliance on the Creator [Khaliq] of the earth and the heavens."

Bahlul the Crazy One [al-Majnun] (may Allah the Exalted bestow His mercy upon him) was once asked: "When does the servant [of the Lord] become someone who is absolutely trustful [mutawakkil]?" To this he replied: "When he, as a person [bi'n-nafs], is a stranger among his fellow creatures, and when, in his inner feeling [bi'l-qalb], he is close to the Truth [al-Haqq]."

Someone asked Hatim al-Asamm ["the Deaf"] (may Allah the Exalted bestow His mercy upon him): "On what basis have you developed this special condition of yours, this absolute trust in the Lord [tawakkul]?" To this he replied: "On four particular elements, namely: (1) I came to realize that my sustenance will not be consumed by anyone other than myself, so I should not be concerned about it; (2) I came to realize that my work will not be done by anyone other than myself, so I must be busy about it; (3) I came to realize that death may come suddenly and unexpectedly, so I must waste no time in order to forestall it; (4) I came to realize that I am in the sight of Allah (Exalted is He) in every condition and circumstance, so I must behave with due modesty under His gaze."

Abu Musa ad-Dabili (may Allah the Exalted bestow His mercy upon him) is reported as having said:

"I asked 'Abd ar-Rahman ibn Yahya about absolute trust in the Lord [tawakkul], so he told me: '[It means that] even if you were to stick your hand into the mouth of the great sea monster [tinnin], as far as the wrist, you would fear nothing other than Allah."

Abu Musa (may Allah the Exalted bestow His mercy upon him) went on to say:

"I then set out to visit Abu Yazid al-Bistami (may Allah the Exalted bestow His mercy upon him), in order to ask him about absolute trust in the Lord [tawakkul]. When I knocked on his door, he said to me: 'O Abu Musa, what did you find unsatisfactory in the answer you received from 'Abd ar-Rahman, that you should come and ask me the same question?' So I said: 'O my master, open the door!' But he said: 'If you were coming to see me as a regular visitor, I would open the door for you. Take your answer from the door!' So I turned away and left [with the answer, which was: 'Absolute trust in the Lord [tawakkul] means that] even if the serpent that is coiled around the Heavenly Throne ['Arsh] were to take an interest in you, you would fear nothing other than Allah.'"

Abu Musa (may Allah the Exalted bestow His mercy upon him) then continued:

"So I kept travelling until I came to [the city of] Dabil, where I took up residence for one whole year. Then I decided it was time to pay a visit, so I set out on the road to Abu Yazid [al-Bistami]. When I reached him, he said to me: 'Now you have come to see me as a regular visitor. Welcome to the visitor! Do come in!' So I stayed as his guest for a month, during which nothing ever occurred to me without his telling me all about it, before I had time to ask him. Then I said to him: 'O Abu Yazid, I now propose to take my leave, so I request you to provide me with a useful lesson.' To this he replied: 'The useful lesson provided by creatures is not a useful lesson!' So I understood this to be a useful lesson, and took my leave."

According to a report from Ibn Tawus al-Yamani (may Allah the Exalted bestow His mercy upon him), his father, Tawus (may Allah the Exalted bestow His mercy upon him), told him:

"An Arab nomad [A'rabi] once came [to Mecca] on a riding camel of his. He caused the beast to kneel down, and hobbled its feet with a cord. Then he raised his head toward the sky, and said: 'O Allah, this riding camel, as well as the load upon its back, is covered by Your insurance, until I return to reclaim it.' He then went off and entered the Sacred Mosque [al-Masjid al-Haram].

Some time later, the Arab nomad returned from the Sacred Mosque [al-Masjid al-Haram]-to find that the riding camel had been taken away, together with the load on its back. So he raised his head toward the sky, and said: 'O Allah, nothing has been stolen from me, for nothing is ever stolen except from You.'"

Tawus went on to say:

"While we were in this situation together with the Arab nomad, we suddenly caught sight of a man descending from the peak of Mount Abu Qubais. He was leading the riding camel with his left hand, while his right hand, which had been cut off, was attached to a cord around his neck. When he eventually reached the Arab nomad, he said: 'Here, take your riding camel, along with the load on its back.'

I asked the man about his condition, so he explained: 'On the peak of Abu Qubais, I was approached by a rider on a grey horse. "O thief," he said to me, "hold out your hand!" So I held it out, and he placed it on a slab of rock. Then he took another piece of rock and used it to amputate my hand, which he then tied to my neck. "Now go back down the mountain," he told me, "and return the riding camel, along with the load it carries, to the Arab nomad."'"

[The Caliph] 'Umar ibn al-Khattab (may Allah be well pleased with him) is reported as having said: "Allah's Messenger (Allah bless him and give him peace) once said:

"'If you really and truly placed all your trust in Allah [law tawakkaltum 'ala'llahi haqqa tawakkuli-hi], He would sustain you as He sustains the birds. They start the day with their bellies empty, and end it with their bellies full.'"

According to a traditional report, transmitted by Muhammad ibn Ka'b on the authority of Ibn 'Abbas (may Allah be well pleased with him and with his father), Allah's Messenger (Allah bless him and give him peace) also said:

If it would please someone to be the noblest of men, let him devote himself truly to Allah. And if it would please someone to be the richest of men, let him be more reliant on what is at the disposal of Allah, and less reliant on what is at his own disposal.

'Umar [ibn al-Khattab] (may Allah be well pleased with him) used to quote these two verses [of Arabic poetry] as an instructive example:

Go easy on yourself, for the outcome of all affairs is determined by God's decree.

If something is meant to go elsewhere, it will never come your way, but if it is yours by destiny, from you it cannot flee.

Someone asked Yahya ibn Mu'adh [ar-Razi] (may Allah the Exalted bestow His mercy upon him): "When does a man become someone who is absolutely trustful [mutawakkil]?" To this he replied: "When he is perfectly satisfied with Allah as a Trustee [Wakil]."

It was Bishr [al-Hafi] (may Allah the Exalted bestow His mercy upon him) who said:

"One of them may say: 'I have put all my trust in Allah [tawakkaltu 'ala'llah],' although he is actually telling a lie. For, by Allah, if he had really put all his trust in Allah, he would be perfectly content with the way Allah treats him."

Abu Turab an-Nakhshabi (may Allah the Exalted bestow His mercy upon him) once said:

"Absolute trust in the Lord [tawakkul] means casting the physical body into servitude ['ubudiyya], attaching the inner feeling to the Divine Lordship [rububiyya], and having serene confidence in sufficiency [kifaya], so that one responds to receiving by giving thanks, and to deprivation by being patient."

It was Dhu 'n-Nun al-Misri [the Egyptian] (may Allah the Exalted bestow His mercy upon him) who said:

"Absolute trust in the Lord [tawakkul] means giving up self-management, and divesting oneself of any personal claim to power and strength."

Dhu'n-Nun (may Allah the Exalted bestow His mercy upon him) also said, to a man who asked him about absolute trust in the Lord [tawakkul]:

"It means detaching oneself from worldly lords [arbab], and severing all attachment to material means [asbab]."

The questioner went on to say: "Tell me more," so he added:

"[It means] throwing the lower self [nafs] into servitude ['ubudiyya], and removing it from the position of lordship [rububiyya]."

He also said: "It means the cessation of ambitious designs [matami']."

As for the enterprising activity that is undertaken with the outer being [al-haraka bi'z-zahir]--which is a way of describing material acquisition [kasb] conducted in accordance with the Sunna --this is not incompatible with the absolute trust experienced by the inner feeling [tawakkul al-qalb], after the servant [of the Lord] has come to realize, within his inner feeling, that the power to decide is the prerogative of Allah (Almighty and Glorious is He). [There is no incompatibility between the two] because the location of absolute trust [tawakkul] is the inner feeling, and because it constitutes the actualization of faith [tahqiq al-iman]. To reject the validity of material acquisition [kasb] would be tantamount to rejecting the validity of the Sunna, and to reject the validity of absolute trust [tawakkul] would be tantamount to rejecting the validity of faith [iman].

If some difficulty is encountered in relation to the material means [asbab], it is due to the decree of Allah (Almighty and Glorious is He), and if something is found to be easy in that regard, it is due to His facilitation (Almighty and Glorious is He). The limbs and organs of the physical body, and all the external faculties [zawahir], must therefore be actively involved in the instrumental process [mutaharrika bi's-sabab], in compliance with the commandment of Allah (Almighty and Glorious is He), while the inner being [batin] remains calmly reliant on the promise of Allah (Almighty and Glorious is He).

Anas ibn Malik (may Allah be well pleased with him) is reported as having said:

"A man once rode into town on a fine she-camel of his, and he said: 'O Messenger of Allah, shall I just leave her unattended, and put my trust in the Lord [ada'u-ha wa atawakkalu]?' So the Prophet (Allah bless him and give him peace) told him: 'Hobble her feet with a rope, and put your trust in the Lord [a'qil-ha wa tawakkal]!'"

In the words of one wise saying:

"He who puts all his trust in the Lord is like a baby. Just as the infant is not aware of having anything else to turn to, except its mother's breast, the completely trustful person [al-mutawakkil] feels himself guided in no other direction, except toward his Lord (Almighty and Glorious is He)."
In the words of another wise saying:

"Absolute trust in the Lord [tawakkul] means the banishment of doubts, and the delegation [tafwid] of one's concerns to the King of kings [Malik al-muluk]."

In the words of yet another wise saying:

"Absolute trust in the Lord [tawakkul] means relying with confidence on what is at the disposal of Allah (Almighty and Glorious is He), and expecting nothing at all from what is at the disposal of human beings."

This saying also deserves to be quoted:

"Absolute trust in the Lord [tawakkul] means emptying the innermost being [sirr] of any consideration one might give to the idea of resorting to litigation [taqadi] in the quest for sustenance."

****

This brings us to the end of the section concerning absolute trust in the Lord [tawakkul].

Praise be to Allah, the Lord of All the Worlds! [al-hamdu li'llahi Rabbi'l-'alamin].

AL-GHUNYA LI-TALIBI TARIQ AL-HAQQ - 4
CONCERNING THANKFULNESS [SHUKR].

As for thankfulness [shukr], the basic guidance on the subject is contained in the words of Allah (Almighty and Glorious is He):

If you are thankful, I will surely give you more; but if you are ungrateful, My punishment is terrible indeed. (14:7)

This is reinforced by the traditional report, transmitted on the authority of 'Ata' (may Allah the Exalted bestow His mercy upon him), who said:

"I entered the presence of [the Prophet's widow] 'A'isha (may Allah be well pleased with her), and said: 'Tell us about the most amazing experience you ever had in the company of Allah's Messenger (Allah bless him and give him peace).' She wept at first, but then she said: 'Was there anything at all about him that was not a marvellous wonder? He came to me one night, and snuggled up beside me in my bed [firashi] until his skin was touching my skin. But then he said: 'O daughter of Abu Bakr, let me go, so that I may devote myself to the worship of my Lord.'

She said: 'So I told him: "I love your nearness, but I prefer to respect your dearest wish." I therefore allowed him (Allah bless him and give him peace) to take his leave of me. So he got up, found a skin container full of water, and performed his ritual ablution [tawadda'a], pouring a considerable amount of water in the process. Then he stood erect, and started to perform the ritual prayer [qama fa-salla]. He wept as he did so, until his tears were streaming down onto his chest. Then he adopted the bowing posture [raka'a], and shed more tears. Then he prostrated himself [sajada], and again he wept. Then he raised his head, and wept still more. He went on like this (Allah bless him and give him peace) until Bilal (may Allah be well pleased with him) arrived on the scene, and so he told him about the ritual prayer [salat].

'I then said: 'O Messenger of Allah, what causes you to weep, when Allah has forgiven you your earlier and later sins?' To this he replied (Allah bless him and give him peace):

'Should I not be a thankful servant ['abd shakur]'? Why should I not do it, since Allah (Almighty and Glorious is He) has sent down to me the words of revelation:

Surely in the creation of the heavens and the earth, and the alternation of night and day, and the ship that runs upon the sea with that which is of use to human beings, and the water which Allah sends down from the sky, thereby reviving the earth after its death, and dispersing all kinds of beasts therein, and the distribution of the winds, and the clouds set in orderly array between heaven and earth--surely there are signs for people who can understand. (2:164)'''

According to those who specialize in ascertaining the actual facts [ahl at-tahqiq], the true nature of thankfulness [haqiqat ash-shukr] is the acknowledgment of the benefaction of the benefactor [ni'mat al-mun'im], with an attitude of humility. In accordance with this meaning, Allah (Exalted is He) has described Himself as being the Most Thankful One [ash-Shakur] in the widest sense, that is to say, in the sense that He rewards His servants for their thankfulness. For the recompense of thankfulness [jaza' ash-shukr] is also called thankfulness [shukr], just as Allah (Almighty and Glorious is He) has said:

And the recompense of an evil is an evil just like it. (42:40)

It has also been said that the true nature of thankfulness [haqiqat ash-shukr] is the act of praising the beneficent person [muhsin] by mentioning his beneficence [ihsan]. The servant's thankfulness [shukr] to Allah (Exalted is He) is therefore expressed through the praise he offers to Him, by mentioning His beneficence [ihsan] toward His servant. As for the thankfulness [shukr] of the Lord of Truth (Glory be to Him) toward His servant, it is expressed through the praise He confers upon him, by making it known that he has acted beneficently for His sake. Furthermore, the beneficence [ihsan] of the servant represents his worshipful obedience to Allah, while the beneficence [ihsan] of the Lord of Truth (Glory be to Him) represents His bestowal of gracious favour [in'am] upon His servant. When the thankfulness [shukr] of the servant is genuine, it is not only a matter of utterance by the tongue, but also the heart's acknowledgment of the Lord's bestowal of gracious favour [in'am ar-Rabb].

Moreover, thankfulness [shukr] can be subdivided into several categories, namely:

1. Thankfulness expressed by the tongue [shukr bi'l-lisan]. This constitutes the acknowledgment of the benefaction [ni'ma] with an attitude of humble acceptance [istikana].

2. Thankfulness expressed by the body and the limbs [shukr bi'l-badan wa'l-arkan]. This is the characteristic indication of loyalty and readiness to serve [al-wafa' wa'l-khidma].

3. Thankfulness expressed by the inner feeling [shukr bi'l-qalb]. This requires a careful balance between the visible display of appreciation and the constant preservation of a sense of reverence.

It has also been said that thankfulness of the eyes [shukr al-'ainain] means that you overlook any fault you notice in your companion, while thankfulness of the ears [shukr al-udhunain] means that you ignore any fault you hear him accused of possessing.

In the simplest terms, thankfulness [shukr] means that you do not disobey Allah (Exalted is He) by misusing His gracious favours.

Here is another saying that clearly deserves to be quoted:

"Thankfulness [shukr] may mean the thankfulness of the learned scholars [shukr al-'alimin], in which case it will be among the subjects they discuss.

Thankfulness [shukr] may mean the thankfulness of the dedicated worshippers [shukr al-'abidin], in which case it will be a feature of their actions.

Thankfulness [shukr] may mean the thankfulness of those who know by direct intuition [shukr al-'arifin], in which case it will be expressed through their honest devotion to Him (Almighty and Glorious is He) in all their states and conditions. It will be expressed through their firm conviction that whatever is good in their experience, and whatever is manifested from them in the way of worshipful obedience, servitude, and remembrance of Him (Almighty and Glorious is He), is entirely due to His enabling guidance [tawfiq], His gracious favour, His help, His power and His strength (Almighty and Glorious is He). It will be expressed through their detachment from all of that, and their total absorption [fana'] in Him. It will be expressed through their acknowledgment of their own inability, deficiency and ignorance, and then through their humble submission to Him (Almighty and Glorious is He) in all conditions and circumstances."

It was Abu Bakr al-Warraq (may Allah the Exalted bestow His mercy upon him) who said:

"Thankfulness for a gracious favour [shukr an-ni'ma] means feasting one's eyes on the gift received, while preserving a sense of reverence."

As someone else once put it:

"Thankfulness for a gracious favour [shukr an-ni'ma] means that you regard yourself as no more deserving of it than a parasite [tufaili]."

It was Abu 'Uthman [al-Hiri] (may Allah the Exalted bestow His mercy upon him) who said:

"Thankfulness [shukr] is the conscious awareness [ma'rifa] of the fact that you are quite incapable of thankfulness."

Let us also consider the following wise sayings:

"Thankfulness for thankfulness [ash-shukr 'ala'sh-shukr] is more complete than simple thankfulness [shukr]. This means that you regard your thankfulness as the result of His enablement [tawfiq], and you have received that enablement on account of the gracious favours bestowed upon you, so you give thanks to Him for the thankfulness He has enabled you to experience. Then you thank Him for the thankfulness-upon-thankfulness [shukr ash-shukr], and so on ad infinitum."

"Thankfulness [shukr] is the attribution of blessings to their Master [Mawla], with an attitude of humble submission to Him."

It was al-Junaid (may Allah the Exalted bestow His mercy upon him) who said:

"Thankfulness [shukr] means that you do not look upon yourself as worthy of the gracious favour you have received." In several wise sayings, the meaning of the simple adjective shakir [thankful; grateful] is contrasted with the significance of the intensive form shakur [very thankful; most grateful; extremely appreciative]. For instance:

"The person who is simply thankful [shakir] is someone who gives thanks for what is available [mawjud], while the person who is very thankful [shakur] is someone who gives thanks for what is unavailable [mafqud]."

"The person who is simply thankful [shakir] is someone who gives thanks for the provision of benefit [naf'], while the person who is very thankful [shakur] is someone who gives thanks for the withholding of benefit [man']."

"The person who is simply thankful [shakir] is someone who gives thanks for the granting of gifts ['ata'], while the person who is very thankful [shakur] is someone who gives thanks for trial and tribulation [bala']."

"The person who is simply thankful [shakir] is someone who gives thanks in response to immediate delivery [badhl], while the person who is very thankful [shakur] is someone who gives thanks when delivery is subject to deferment [matl]."

It was [Abu Bakr ibn Jahdar] ash-Shibli (may Allah the Exalted bestow His mercy upon him) who said:

"Thankfulness [shukr] means focusing attention on the source of the benefit [mun'im], not focusing attention on the benefit [ni'ma] itself."

Someone else had this to say on the subject:

"Thankfulness [shukr] means firmly securing the bonds of that which has been found [qaid al-mawjud], and then hunting for that which is still missing [said al-mafqud]."

It was Abu 'Uthman [al-Hiri] (may Allah the Exalted bestow His mercy upon him) who said:

"The thankfulness of the common folk [shukr al-'amma] is for food and drink and clothing, while the thankfulness of the elite [shukr al-khawass] is for the spiritual values [ma'ani] conferred upon their hearts."

Allah (Almighty and Glorious is He) has told us:

And few of My servants are very thankful. (34:13)

[The Prophet] David (peace be upon him) once said:

"My God [Ilahi], how can I thank You, when my thankfulness to You [shukri la-ka] is itself a blessing from among Your gracious favours [ni'ma min ni'ami-ka]?"

So Allah (Blessed and Exalted is He) conveyed to him by way of inspiration [awha ilai-h]: "Now you have thanked Me indeed! [al-ana qad shakarta-ni]."

To quote another wise saying:

"If your hand is too short to extend remuneration, let your tongue dwell at length on the expression of thanks [shukr]."

When Idris (peace be upon him) was given the good tiding of forgiveness, he is said to have asked for life. "Why?" he was asked, so he explained: "So that I may be able to thank Him, for I was previously working for forgiveness." The angel thereupon spread its wing, and carried him up to heaven.

It is said that one of the Prophets [Anbiya'] (peace be upon them all) once passed by a small stone, from which a large amount of water was gushing forth. He was astonished at the sight, but Allah caused the stone to let him know that it could speak, so he asked it about its condition. It told him: "Ever since I heard Allah (Almighty and Glorious is He) speak of:

A Fire of which the fuel is men and stones. (66:6)

I have been weeping from fear of it." So that Prophet (peace be upon him) offered a prayer of supplication, pleading with Him to grant that stone asylum from the Fire. Allah (Almighty and Glorious is He) thereupon conveyed to him by way of inspiration [awha ilai-h]: "I have already granted it asylum from the Fire." That Prophet then continued on his way. When he returned later on, he found that the water was still gushing from the stone, but even more copiously than on his previous visit. He was bewildered, but Allah (Exalted is He) again caused the stone to let him know that it could speak, so he said to it: "Why are you still weeping, when Allah has already forgiven you?" The stone explained: "That was the weeping of sorrow and fear, but this is the weeping of thankfulness [shukr] and joy."

In the words of another wise saying:

"One who is thankful [shakir] is in the presence of superabundance [mazid], because he is going through the experience of receiving gracious favour [ni'ma], for Allah (Exalted is He) has told us:

If you are thankful, I will surely give you more. (14:7)

And one who is patient [sabir] is in the presence of Allah, taking shelter with Him (Exalted is He), because he is going through the experience of suffering trial and tribulation [bala']. Allah (Exalted is He) has told us:

Surely Allah is with those who are patient. (2:153)"

"Praise [hamd]," it has been said, "is for the very breaths we breathe, while thankfulness [shukr] is for the blessings of the senses."

In the words of the authentic tradition [al-khabar as-sahih]:

The first of those invited to enter the Garden of Paradise will be those who are constantly praising Allah [al-hammaduna li'llah].

"Praise [hamd]," it has also been said, "is for what He has prevented, while thankfulness [shukr] is for what He has brought into being."

The following story was told by one of the righteous:

"In the course of one of my journeys, I caught sight of an old man, who was far advanced in age, so I asked him about his condition. He responded by telling me: 'In the early part of my life, I was deeply in love with a cousin of mine, the daughter of my paternal uncle, and she was equally in love with me, so it was agreed that I should marry her. [When she entered my chamber] on the night of her bridal procession [zifaf], I said to her: 'Come, let us spend the whole of this night in worship, as a way of giving thanks to Allah [shukran li'llah] (Almighty and Glorious is He) for having brought us together.' So we performed the ritual prayer [sallaina] throughout that night, and neither of us paid any attention to the other. Then, when the second night came around, we spent the whole of it in similar fashion. This came to be our constant practice, so that now, after seventy or eighty years have gone by, we are still in that same state every night.' His wife was with him at the time, so he turned to her and asked her: 'Is that not just the way it is, O So-and-so?' To this the old woman replied: 'It is just as the old man told you.'"

****

This brings us to the end of the section concerning thankfulness [shukr].

Praise be to Allah, the Lord of All the Worlds! [al-hamdu li'llahi Rabbi'l-'alamin].

AL-GHUNYA·LI-TALIBI TARIQ AL-HAQQ - 5
A SERIES OF INVOCATIONS, EACH OF THEM BEGINNING WITH: "IN THE NAME OF ALLAH, WHO [BISMI'LLAHI'LLADHI]."

Say: "In the Name of Allah, who utterly transcends any attribution of counterparts [addad]. In the Name of Allah, who is absolutely exempt from any attribution of partners or peers [andad]. In the Name of Allah, who is far removed in His Holiness from the begetting of children [awlad].

"In the Name of Allah, who causes all lights to shine [nawwara'l-anwar]. In the Name of Allah, who honours those who are righteous and fine [abrar]. In the Name of Allah, who has predetermined all destinies [aqdar], and who has enlightened human hearts and eyes [absar].

In the Name of Allah, who manifests Himself to the hearts of the righteous [abrar] in those moments just before the break of day [ashar]. "In the Name of Allah, who allows dear friends to gain knowledge of the mysteries [asrar], for He floods them with rays of light [anwar] and entrusts them with the keeping of those secrets [asrar]. From them He banishes all dangers [akhtar]. He preserves them from being enslaved by jealous rivals [aghyar], and He relieves them of all burdens, shackles, bonds [asar] and heavy loads [awzar].

For indeed, He has been characterized from all eternity by the attributes of beneficence, abundant grace, and readiness to forgive the sins of those who seek forgiveness [ahl al-istighfar]."

Say: "In the Name of Allah, the Name of the One who causes the flowing of the rivers [anhar] and the sprouting of the trees [ashjar]." [Say: "In the Name of Allah," for that is] the Name of the One who brings prosperity to countries and towns by populating them with truly obedient folk from among His servants ['ibad]. Such people serve as mainstays [awtad], as mountain-like pillars of support, so that, for those who dwell upon it, the earth comes to be as safe and as cosy as the cradle [mihad]. They are the Forty, the pick of the spiritual deputies [abdal], the ones who never let it be forgotten that the Lord is totally exempt from any attribution of partners and peers [andad]. They are kings in this world, and they will be intercessors on behalf of humankind upon the Day of the Final Summoning [Yawm at-Tanad]. My Lord has indeed created them as a benefit to all the world, and as a gift of mercy to His servants ['ibad].

On some of the many precious blessings conferred by "In the Name of Allah [Bismi'llah]."

"In the Name of Allah [Bismi'llah]" is a treasure for those who remember, a mighty resource for the strong, a protective talisman for the weak, a radiant light for lovers, and a joyful delight for those who are filled with yearning.

"In the Name of Allah [Bismi'llah]" is the consolation of our spiritual natures [arwah]. "In the Name of Allah [Bismi'llah]" is the salvation of our bodily forms [ashbah]. "In the Name of Allah [Bismi'llah]" is the light that illuminates our breasts [sudur]. "In the Name of Allah [Bismi'llah]" is the organizing principle that regulates our affairs [umur]. "In the Name of Allah [Bismi'llah]" is the crown of the truly confident [taj al-wathiqin]. "In the Name of Allah [Bismi'llah]" is the lamp of those who reach their destination [siraj al-wasilin]. "In the Name of Allah [Bismi'llah]" is that which satisfies the needs of ardent lovers [mughni'l-'ashiqin]. "In the Name of Allah [Bismi'llah]" is the Name of the One who honours certain servants and humiliates certain servants ['ibad].

"In the Name of Allah [Bismi'llah]" is the Name of the One who keeps the Fire of Hell in store for His enemies as an ambush [mirsad], and who keeps the Beatific Vision in store for His friends as a promised rendezvous [mi 'ad]. "In the Name of Allah [Bismi'llah]" is the Name of the Single One without number [Wahid bi-la 'adad]. "In the Name of Allah [Bismi'llah]" is the Name of the One who endures forever without end [al-Baqi bi-la amad]. "In the Name of Allah [Bismi'llah]" is the Name of the One who stands firm without supporting props [Qa'im bi-la 'amad]. "In the Name of Allah [Bismi'llah]" is the invocation that serves as an introduction [iftitah] to every Sura [of the Qur'an].

It is the Name of the One who brings good cheer to those who practice solitary retreats [khalawat]. It is the Name of the One who brings a sense of completeness to those who perform the ritual prayers [salawat]. It is the Name of the One who inspires us to improve our minds by thinking better thoughts [Dunun]. It is the Name of the One for whose sake we spend the night with sleepless eyes ['uyun]. It is the Name of the One who has only to say to something, "Be!" and there it is [yakun]. It is the Name of the One who is far beyond description in terms of physical touch [misas]. It is the Name of the One who can dispense entirely with human beings [unas]. It is the Name of the One who rises majestically above all comparison [qiyas].

Say: "In the Name of Allah [Bismi'llah]" letter by letter [harfan harfa], for then you will receive the recompense in multiples of a thousand [alfan alfa], and the burdens of sin will be scooped away from you by the shovelful [jarfan jarfa]. If someone says it with his tongue, that person will witness all that is offered by this world [dunya]. If someone says it with his heart, that person will witness all that is offered by the world hereafter ['uqba]. And if someone says it with his innermost being, that person will actually witness the Master [Mawla].

"In the Name of Allah [Bismi'llah]" is a phrase that brings a pleasant sensation to the mouth [fam]. "In the Name of Allah [Bismi'llah]" is a phrase with which no feeling of unhappiness [ghamm] can coexist. It is a phrase that brings about the perfection of good fortune [ni'ma]. It is a phrase that brings about the abolition of misfortune [niqma]. It is a phrase that accounts for the special privileges enjoyed by this [the Islamic] Community [Umma].

To utter the whole phrase, "In the Name of Allah, the All-Merciful, the All-Compassionate [Bismi'llahi'r-Rahmani'r-Rahim]," is to pronounce a simultaneous invocation of Divine Majesty [Jalal] and Divine Beauty [Jamal], for "In the Name of Allah [Bismi'llah]" is an invocation of Divine Majesty within an expression of majesty [Jalal fi jalal], while "the All-Merciful, the All-Compassionate [ar-Rahmani'r-Rahim]" is an invocation of Divine Beauty within an expression of beauty [Jamal fi jamal].

Those who witness His Majesty are likely to lose their wits [tasha]; whereas those who witness His Beauty are sure to prosper ['asha]. The whole phrase represents a simultaneous invocation of Divine Power [Qudra] and Divine Mercy [Rahma], whereby the Divine Power adds together all the acts of obedience performed by the obedient [muti'in], while the Divine Mercy erases all the sins committed by the sinners [mudhnibin].

Concerning the progressive stages of spiritual development that stem from the invocation: "In the Name of Allah [Bismi'llah]."

Say: "In the Name of Allah [Bismi'llah]," for [when you pronounce these words of His] it is as if He is saying: "With My help, a person arrives at the stage where he is capable of performing meaningful acts of worshipful obedience. Then, by the light of those acts of worshipful obedience, he moves on until he reaches the stage of direct witnessing ['iyan], at which point he is able to dispense with second-hand explanation [bayan]. His heart has now become a vessel worthy of containing both the esoteric mysteries and the exoteric branches of religious knowledge ['ulum al-adyan]."

"When someone attains to the Loving Friend [Habib], he is safely delivered from woe and lamentation [nahib]. When someone attains to unfiltered vision [nazar], he has no further use for hearsay information [khabar]. When someone attains to the Everlasting Lord [as-Samad], he is safely delivered from grief and sorrow [kamad]. When someone attains to close companionship [rifaq], he is safely delivered from lonely separation [firaq]. When someone attains to noble dignity [majd], he ceases to be affected by emotional upheaval [wajd]. And when someone attains to the Ultimate Meeting [Liqa'], he is rendered immune to painful suffering [shaqa']."

Some further interpretations of the Arabic letters and words that occur in: "Bismi'llahi'r-Rahmani'r-Rahim [In the Name of Allah, the All-Merciful, the All-Compassionate]."

Say: "Bismi'llah [In the Name of Allah]." According to one interpretation, the letter ba' stands for Bari' al-baraya [the Maker of all creatures], while the letter sin stands for Sattar al-khataya [the Veiler of faults], and the letter mim stands for al-Mannan bi'l-'ataya [the Bestower of gifts].

There are some who maintain that the letter ba' stands for Bar[i'] min al-awlad [the One who is Exempt from begetting children], while the letter sin stands for Sami' al-aswat [the Hearer of the voices (that appeal to Him)], and the letter mim stands for Mujib ad-da'awat [the One who responds to prayers of supplication].

According to another interpretation, the significance of these three letters [in reverse order] is expressed by the following commands of the Lord: "Offer food to your fellow creatures, for I am the One who provides you with food [Mut'imukum]. Offer them water to drink, for I am the One who quenches your thirst [Saqikum]. Pay attention to Me, for I am your Eternal Lord [Baqikum]."

Still others maintain that the letter ba' stands for buka' at-ta'ibin [the weeping of those who repent], while the letter sin stands for sujud al-'abidin [the act of prostration made by worshippers (in their ritual prayer)], and the letter mim stands for ma'dhirat al-mudhnibin [the pardoning of sinners].

Turning from letter-by-letter to word-by-word interpretations, we find that some have explained the nuances of meaning as follows: Allah is the Remover of trials and tribulations [Allahu Kashif al-balaya]. The All-Merciful is the Giver of gifts [ar-Rahmanu Mu'ti'l-'ataya]. The All-Compassionate is the Forgiver of faults [ar-Rahimu Ghafir al-khataya]. "Allah" is for those who know by intuition [Allahu li'l-'arifin]. "The All-Merciful" is for devout worshippers [ar-Rahmanu li'l-'abidin]. "The All-Compassionate" is for sinners [ar-Rahimu li'l-mudhnibin].

Allah is the One who created you all, and He is the Most Excellent of Creators [Ahsan al-Khaliqin]. The All-Merciful [ar-Rahman] is the One who provides for you all, and He is the Best of Providers [Khair ar-Raziqin]. The All-

Compassionate [ar-Rahim] is the One who is ready to forgive you all, and He is the Best of Forgivers [Khair al-Ghafirin].

We also encounter this alternative explanation:

He is "Allah" from the standpoint of the actual process of bestowing lavish blessings [Allahu bi-isbagh an-ni'am], and He is "the All-Merciful, the All-Compassionate" with regard to the qualities of magnanimity and generosity [ar-Rahman ar-Rahim bi'l-jud wa'l-karam]. He is "Allah" by virtue of the fact that He brings us forth from our mothers' wombs [butun]. He is "the All-Merciful [ar-Rahman]" by virtue of the fact that He brings us forth from our graves [qubur]. He is "the All-Compassionate [ar-Rahim]" by virtue of the fact that He brings us forth from the depths of darkness into the light [nur].

Concerning some particular benefits obtained by those who invoke the Divine Mercy by saying: "In the Name of Allah [Bismi'llah]."

Allah will surely bestow His mercy upon those who refuse to follow Satan [Shaitan], who turn away from sinful disobedience ['isyan], who take good care to avoid the Fires of Hell [niran], who make it their regular practice to perform works of charity [ihsan], and who constantly remember the All-Merciful [ar-Rahman], for they never fail to invoke His Mercy by saying: "In the Name of Allah [Bismi'llah]."

Allah will surely bestow His Mercy upon those who take refuge with Allah, who turn in repentance to Allah, who put their absolute trust in Allah, and who actively practice the remembrance of Allah, for they never fail to invoke His Mercy by saying: "In the Name of Allah [Bismi'llah]."

Allah will surely bestow His Mercy upon those who abstain from this world [dunya], who long for the hereafter, who endure with patience when they must suffer pain [adha], who give thanks for blessed well-being [na'ma'], and who actively practice the remembrance of the Master [Mawla], for they never fail to invoke His Mercy by saying: "In the Name of Allah [Bismi'llah]."

Congratulations to any servant [of Allah] who is steering well clear of the Tempter [Taghut], who is expecting nothing more from this world than his basic nourishment [qut], and who is actively practicing the remembrance of the Living One who never dies [al-Hayy alladhi la yamut], for that servant is surely saying right now:

"In the Name of Allah [Bismi'llah]."

AL-GHUNYA LI-TALIBI TARIQ AL-HAQQ - 6 CONCERNING THE RITUAL PRAYER OF THE SPIRITUAL ELITE [SALAT AL-KHASSA].

As for the ritual prayer of the spiritual elite [salat al-khassa], it serves to alert the wakeful, the humbly submissive, the vigilant, the guardians of hearts, the welcome guests of the All-Merciful [ar-Rahman] (may they enjoy the good pleasure of Allah, and may His peace be upon them all). A good description of it is related in the following report:

Yusuf ibn 'Isam was passing through one of the large congregational mosques [jami' min jawami'] of Khurasan, when he came across an enormous circle [halqa] of people. He stopped to ask someone about it, and he was told: "That is the circle of Hatim. He is speaking on the subjects of abstinence [zuhd] and pious caution [wara'], and about fear and hope." Yusuf then turned to his companions and said: "Come on, let us ask him a question on the subject of the ritual prayer [salat]! Then, if he gives us a satisfying answer, we shall sit with him and join his circle."

He thereupon went up to Hatim, saluted him with the greeting of peace [sallama 'alai-hi], and said:

"May Allah bestow His mercy upon you [rahima-ka'llah]! I have a question I wish to put to you."

"Go ahead and ask it," said Hatim, and the following conversation then took place between the two of them:

Yusuf said: "I wish to ask you about the ritual prayer [salat]."

Hatim said: "Do you wish to ask me about its significance as a spiritual experience [ma'rifa], or about the discipline [adab] to be observed in its performance? There are two distinct questions here, requiring two separate answers."

Yusuf said: "In that case, let me ask you about the discipline [adab] to be observed in its performance."

Hatim said: "It means that you rise to the occasion, and walk [to the place of worship] with an attitude of total dedication [ihtisab]. It means that you begin the actual prayer with the appropriate intention [niyya], and pronounce the declaration of Allah's Supreme Greatness [by saying 'Allahu Akbar'] in a spirit of glorification [tukabbiru bi't-ta'zim]. It means that you recite [from the Qur'an] with a clear and distinct enunciation [tartil]. It means that you perform the act of bowing with humility [tarka'u bi'l-khushu'], the act of prostration with submissiveness [tasjudu bi't-tawadu'], the testimony with sincerity [tatashahhadu bi'l-ikhlas], and the salutation with a feeling of compassion [tusallimu bi'r-rahma]."

Yusuf's companions then prompted him to ask about its significance as a spiritual experience [ma'rifa], so he went ahead and asked this second question, to which Hatim responded by explaining:

"It means that you set the Garden of Paradise to your right, the Fire of Hell to your left, the Bridge [as-Sirat] beneath your feet, and the Balance [al-Mizan] beneath your eyes, and [that you worship] the Lord as if you could see Him, for, even if you do not see Him, He does see you."

"O young man [ya shabb]," said Yusuf, "how long have you been performing this kind of ritual prayer [salat]?"

"For twenty years," said Hatim.

Yusuf said to his companions: "Come now, let us commit ourselves to perform such a prayer [salat] for the next fifty years!" Then he turned to Hatim and asked him: "Where did you find out about this?"

Hatim replied: "From those books of yours, which you used to dictate to us!"

The traditional report [hadith] of Abu Hazim al-A'raj ["the Lame"] (may Allah bestow His mercy upon him) is highly relevant to this whole topic, so we shall now proceed to recount it. To quote the actual words of Abu Hazim al-A'raj (may Allah bestow His mercy upon him):

"One day, while I was at the seashore, one of the Companions of Allah's Messenger (Allah bless him and give him peace) came up to me and said: 'O Abu Hazim, do you know how to perform the ritual prayer [a-tuhsinu an tusalliya]?'

"'How could I not know how to perform the ritual prayer,' said I, 'since I am thoroughly familiar with its strictly obligatory elements [fara'id], as well as with the customary observances [ma'stanna] established by Allah's Messenger (Allah bless him and give him peace)?'"

"'O Abu Hazim,' he then said to me, 'what is required of you, as an obligatory duty [fard], before you stand ready to perform the ritual prayer [salat]?'"

"'There are six requirements,' I replied."

"'What are they?' he asked.'"

"I said: 'They are (1) a state of ritual purity [tahara], (2) covering oneself [to conceal the private parts] [istitar], (3) choosing a suitable spot on which to perform the prayer [ikhtiyar mawdi' as-salat], (4) standing ready to perform the prayer [al-qiyam ila 's-salat], (5) formulating the intention [niyya], and (6) facing toward the Qibla [direction of the Ka'ba in Mecca].'"

"'O Abu Hazim,' he asked me next, 'with what intention [niyya] do you set out from your house toward the mosque [masjid]?'"

"I said: 'With the intention to visit [the place of worship] [bi-niyyat az-ziyara].'"

"He said: 'With what intention [niyya] do you enter the mosque [masjid]?'"

"I said: 'With the intention to perform an act of worship [bi-niyyat al-'ibada].'"

"He said: 'With what intention [niyya] do you stand ready to perform the ritual prayer [salat]?'"

"I said: 'With the intention of servitude [bi-niyyat al-'ubudiyya], acknowledging the state of servitude to Him.'"

Abu Hazim (may Allah bestow His mercy upon him) then continued his account of his conversation with the Companion of the Prophet (Allah bless him and give him peace):

"He came closer to me, and said: 'O Abu Hazim, with what do you confront the Qibla?'"

"I said: 'With three obligatory observances [fara'id] and one customary practice [sunna].'"

"He said: 'And what are they?'"

"I said: 'Facing toward the Qibla is an obligatory observance [fard]. Formulating the intention [niyya] is an obligatory observance [fard]. The initial declaration of Allah's Supreme Greatness [at-takbirat al-ula] is also an obligatory observance [fard]. The act of raising the hands is a customary practice [sunna].'"

"He said: 'In how many instances is pronouncing the declaration of Allah's Supreme Greatness [takbir] required of you as an obligatory observance [fard], and how often as a customary practice [sunna]?'"

"I said: 'The basic principle of takbir [the affirmation of the Supreme Greatness of Allah] is expressed through ninety-four takbira's [utterances of the declaration: "Allahu Akbar (Allah is Supremely Great!)"]. Five of these are strictly obligatory [fard], while all the rest of them are customary [sunna].'"

"He said: 'With what do you mark the opening of the ritual prayer [bi-ma tastaftihu's-salat]?'"

"I said: 'With the affirmation of Allah's Supreme Greatness [bi't-takbir].'"

"He said: 'And what [element of the prayer] is its manifest proof [burhan]?'"

"I said: 'Its Qur'anic recitation [qira'a].'"

"He said: 'And what is its jewel, its very essence [jawhar]?'"

"I said: 'Its glorification [of the Lord] [tasbih].'"

"He said: 'And what is its animation [ihya']?'"

"I said: 'Its humble submission [khushu'].'"

"He said: 'And what is its humble submission [khushu']?'"

"I said: 'Fixing one's gaze on the spot where the act of prostration [sujud] is to be performed.'"

"He said: 'And what is its solemn dignity [waqar]?'"

"I said: 'Its state of calm tranquillity [sukun].'"

"He said: 'And what is its consecration [tahrim]?'"

"I said: 'The [initial] declaration of Allah's Supreme Greatness [takbir].'"

"He said: 'And what is its deconsecration [tahlil]?'"

"I said: 'The [concluding] salutation [taslim].'"

"He said: 'And what is its emblem [shi'ar]?'"

"I said: 'The glorification [of the Lord] [tasbih] when its performance has been duly completed.'"

"He said: 'And what is the key to all of that, O Abu Hazim?'"

"I said: 'The ritual ablution [wudu'].'"

"He said: 'And what is the key to the ritual ablution [miftah al-wudu']?'"

"I said: 'The invocation of Allah's Name [tasmiya].'"

"He said: 'And what is the key to the invocation of Allah's Name [miftah at-tasmiya]?'"

"I said: 'The intention [niyya].'"

"He said: 'And what is the key to the intention [miftah an-niyya]?'"

"I said: 'Certitude [yaqin].'"

"He said: 'And what is the key to certitude [miftah al-yaqin]?'"

"I said: 'Absolute trust [in the Lord] [tawakkul].'"

"He said: 'And what is the key to absolute trust [miftah at-tawakkul]?'"

"I said: 'Fear [khawf].'"

"He said: 'And what is the key to fear [miftah al-khawf]?'"

"I said: 'Hope [raja'].'"

"He said: 'And what is the key to hope [miftah ar-raja']?'"

"I said: 'Patience [sabr].'"

"He said: 'And what is the key to patience [miftah as-sabr]?'"

"I said: 'Contentment [rida].'"

"He said: 'And what is the key to contentment [miftah ar-rida]?'"

"I said: 'Worshipful obedience [ta'a].'"

"He said: 'And what is the key to worshipful obedience [miftah at-ta'a]?'"

"I said: 'Acknowledgment [of truth and reality] [i'tiraf].'"

"He said: 'And what is the key to acknowledgment [of truth and reality] [miftah al-i'tiraf]?'"

"I said: 'Acknowledgment of the Divine Oneness and Lordship [al-i'tiraf bi'l-wahdaniyya wa'r-rububiyya].'"

"He said: 'And by what means did you become acquainted with all of that?'"

"I said: 'Through knowledge ['ilm].'"

"He said: 'And by what means did you acquire knowledge ['ilm]?'"

"I said: 'Through the process of learning [ta'allum].' He said: 'And by what means did you pursue the process of learning [ta'allum]?'"

"I said: 'Through intelligence ['aql].'"

"He said: 'And by what means did you acquire intelligence ['aql]?'"

"I said: 'There are two kinds of intelligence [al-'aql 'aqlan]. For the making of one kind of intelligence, Allah is solely responsible, to the exclusion of His creatures. The other kind of intelligence is one that human beings can develop, through the discipline of training and education. When the two kinds are combined together as a team, each of them assists and supports the other.'"

"He said: 'And by what means did you accomplish all of that?'"

"I said: 'Through the enabling grace [of Allah] [tawfiq]. May Allah enable us, and you, to succeed in achieving that which is worthy of love and approval.'"

"Then he said: 'By Allah, you have already perfected the keys to the Garden of Paradise! So let me hear your answers to the following questions:

(1) What is the obligatory duty [fard] that you must perform?

(2) What is the obligatory duty of the obligatory duty [fard al-fard]?

(3) What is an obligatory duty that leads to an obligatory duty [fard yu'addi ila fard]?

(4) What is the customary practice [sunna] that is included within the obligatory duty [fard]?

(5) What is a customary practice [sunna] by which the obligatory duty [fard] is completed?'"

"I answered his questions as follows:

(1) As for the obligatory duty [fard], that is the ritual prayer [salat].

(2) As for the obligatory duty of the obligatory duty [fard al-fard], that is the state of ritual purity [tahara].

(3) As for an obligatory duty that leads to an obligatory duty [fard yu'addi ila fard], that refers to your taking water in your right hand, and using it to wash your left hand.

(4) As for the customary practice [sunna] that is included within the obligatory duty [fard], that refers to your making water flow between your fingers and toes [when performing the ritual ablution].

(5) As for a customary practice [sunna] by which the obligatory duty [fard] is completed, that is circumcision [khitan]."

"He said: 'You have not left yourself vulnerable to any charge that might be brought against you, O Abu Hazim!'"

AL-GHUNYA LI-TALIBI TARIQ AL-HAQQ - 7 CONCERNING THE NECESSITY TO BE CONSTANTLY ON GUARD AGAINST HYPOCRITICAL DISPLAY [RIYA'], THE DESIRE TO IMPRESS ONE'S FELLOW CREATURES [RU'YAT AL-KHALQ], AND VAIN CONCEIT ['UJB].

It is most important for every devout worshipper [muta'abbid] and truly experienced believer ['arif] to be constantly on guard, in all his conditions and circumstances, against hypocritical display [riya'], the desire to impress his fellow creatures [ru'yat al-khalq], and vain conceit ['ujb]. This is because the lower self [nafs] is malign. It is the source of misleading desires, pernicious appetites, and lustful passions that form a barrier between the servant and the Lord of Truth (Almighty and Glorious is He). There is no road to safety from its wicked and mischievous ways, as long as the spirit [ruh] resides within the body of a human being [ibn Adam].

This is still the case, even if the servant [of the Lord] attains to the state of Spiritual Deputyship [Badaliyya] and Championship of the Truth [Siddiqiyya], although this state is safer than the initial stage of spiritual development, and more secure from the wickedness and the cunning wiles of the lower self [nafs]. In this state, the good is more predominant, the light is more prevalent, the guidance is positively in the direction of Allah's path [fi sabili'llah], the enabling grace [tawfiq] is comprehensive, and the needed protection is always available. Impeccable virtue ['isma] is not for us, however. That is a quality peculiar to the Prophets [Anbiya'] (peace be upon them all), conferred on them in order to draw the distinction between Prophetship [Nubuwwa] and saintship [wilaya]. Allah (Almighty and Glorious is He) has issued a warning threat to those who practice hypocritical display [riya'] and seek to promote an undeserved reputation [sum'a]. He has cautioned us against the wicked inclination of the lower self [nafs] and its mischievous tricks. He has forbidden us to follow its dictates, and He has instructed us to oppose and contradict it, sometimes in the Qur'an, and at other times in the utterances of Allah's Messenger (Allah bless him and give him peace), which are recorded in the traditional reports [akhbar] and enshrined in the Sunna. Let us first consider some examples from the Qur'an [and other Scriptures]: Allah (Almighty and Glorious is He) has said:

So woe to those who pray, but are heedless of their prayers, and to those who make a show, yet withhold the smallest charity. (107:4,5)

He has said (Glorious and Exalted is He):

They utter with their mouths what is not in their hearts. Allah is best aware of what they hide. (3:167)

He has said (Exalted is He):

The hypocrites seek to beguile Allah but it is He who beguiles them. When they stand up to perform the prayer, they perform it languidly and to impress people, and they are mindful of Allah but little.

[They are] swaying between this [and that], belonging neither to these nor to those. If Allah causes someone to go astray, you will not find a way for him. (4:142,143)

He has said (Exalted is He):

O you who believe, many of the [Jewish] rabbis and the [Christian] monks devour the wealth of mankind wantonly, and debar [men] from the way of Allah. (9:34)

He has said (Almighty and Glorious is He):

O you who believe, why do you say that which you do not do? It is most hateful in the sight of Allah that you say what you do not do. (61:2)

He has said (Exalted is He):

Keep your words private or speak openly; He knows what the breasts contain. (67:13)

He has said (Glorious and Exalted is He):

So whoever hopes for the meeting with his Lord, let him do righteous work, and let him give no one any share at all in the worship due unto his Lord. (18:110)

He has said (Exalted is He):

Surely the self is always inciting to evil, except inasmuch as my Lord has mercy. (12:53)

He has said (Exalted is He):

But greed has been made present in the souls [of men]. (4:128)

He said (Almighty and Glorious is He) to David [Dawud] (peace be upon him) [in a non-Qur'anic utterance]:

O David, you must flee from your passionate desire [hawa], for no contender challenges Me for My dominion, apart from passionate desire.

He has also said (Exalted is He):

Do not follow passionate desire, lest it lead you astray from Allah's path. (38:26)

As for the Sunna, Shaddad ibn Aws (may Allah be well pleased with him) is reported as having said: "I once entered the presence of the Prophet (Allah bless him and give him peace), and I noticed a look in his face that made me shudder, so I said: 'What is the matter with you, O Messenger of Allah?' He replied (Allah bless him and give him peace):

"'I am afraid that my Community [Ummati] may be guilty of shirk [attributing partners to Allah], after I am gone.'"

On hearing this, I exclaimed: 'Do you really mean to say, O Messenger of Allah, that they will attribute partners to Him [yushrikuna] after you are gone?' So he went on to explain (Allah bless him and give him peace):

"'They may not worship a sun, or a moon, or a graven image [wathan], or a stone idol, but they will resort to hypocritical display in their religious practices [a'mal], and hypocritical display [riya'] is tantamount to shirk [attributing partners to Allah].'"

"Then he recited the words of Allah (Exalted is He):

So whoever hopes for the meeting with his Lord, let him do righteous work, and let him give no one any share at all in the worship due unto his Lord. (18:110)"

The Prophet (Allah bless him and give him peace) once said:

The Day of Resurrection [Yawm al-Qiyama] will come with sealed scrolls [suhuf makhtuma] [in which the deeds of mankind have been recorded], so Allah (Almighty and Glorious is He) will say to the angels: "Throw this one away, and accept this one." They will respond by saying: "By Your Might and Your Majesty, we know nothing but good." So He will say (Exalted is He): "Yes, but this is [the record of] a deed performed for someone other than Me, and I only accept what was done for the sake of My countenance."

The Prophet (Allah bless him and give him peace) used to say, in his prayer of supplication [du'a']: O Allah, make my tongue pure and free from lying, my heart from hypocrisy [nifaq], my religious practice from hypocritical display [riya'], and my eyesight from treachery, for You know the treachery of the eyes, and what the breasts conceal.

He once said (Allah bless him and give him peace):

You must not sit at the feet of a religious scholar ['alim], unless he summons you away from five toward five, namely: (1) away from indulgence [raghba], in the direction of abstinence [zuhd]; (2) away from hypocritical display [riya'], in the direction of sincere devotion [ikhlas]; (3) away from arrogant pride [kibr], in the direction of modest humility [tawadu']; (4) away from fawning flattery [mudahana], in the direction of honest advice [munasaha]; and (5) away from ignorance [jahl], in the direction of knowledge ['ilm].

He once said (Allah bless him and give him peace):

Allah (Exalted is He) says: "I am the Best Partner [Ana Khairu Sharik]. If someone associates a partner with Me, in his undertaking, it involves the partner ascribed to Me [shariki] and has nothing to do with Me. I accept only that which is devoted solely to Me. O Children of Adam, I am the Best Participant [Ana Khairu Qasim], so reconsider that work of yours, which you have performed for someone other than Me, because your wage is incumbent only on the one for whom you did the work."

He also said (Allah bless him and give him peace):

You may congratulate this Community [Umma] on their brilliance and high standing in the sphere of religion, and on their empowerment in the countries of the earth, so long as they do not perform the work of the hereafter for the sake of this world. If anyone does the work of the hereafter for the sake of this world, it will not be accepted of him, and in the hereafter he will have no share.

He also said (Allah bless him and give him peace):

Allah will surely grant the benefits of this world [for work performed] with the intention of gaining the benefits of the hereafter, but He will not grant the benefits of the hereafter [for work performed] with the intention of gaining the benefits of this world.

As reported on the authority of Anas ibn Malik (may Allah be well pleased with him), Allah's Messenger (Allah bless him and give him peace) once said:

On the night when I was taken on my Heavenly Journey [usriya bi], I passed by a group of people whose lips had been snipped by scissors of fire. "Who are these?" I said to Gabriel (peace be upon him), so he told me: "They are the preachers [khutaba'] of your Community. They say something, but they do not put it into practice. They say what they acknowledge as being correct, but they do what they denounce as being wrong. They instruct the people to act righteously, but they forget to include themselves."

He also said (Allah bless him and give him peace):

The worst of my fears for my Community [Ummati] is every hypocrite [munafiq] with a clever tongue. By the One who holds my soul in His hand, the Final Hour will not come about until they find themselves subject to dishonest rulers, immoral ministers, treacherous assistants, iniquitous professors ['urafa'], dissolute Qur'an-reciters [qurra'], and ignorant servants. Allah (Exalted is He) will expose them to dark and murky intrigue, so they will experience a bewildering perplexity [tahawwuk], like that which afflicted the wrongdoing Jews [Yahud]. From that point on, Islam will unravel, knot by knot, until no one says: "Allah, Allah!"

As reported on the authority of 'Adi ibn Hatim (may Allah be well pleased with him), Allah's Messenger (Allah bless him and give him peace) once said:

"On the Day of Resurrection [Yawm al-Qiyama], certain people will be subjected to exemplary punishment of the most extreme kind. Allah (Exalted is He) will say to them: 'When you were in private situations, you would brazenly affront Me with heinous sins ['aza'im], but when you met with other people, you would approach them modestly and humbly. You were in awe of other people, but you did not regard Me with awe. You honoured other people, but you did not honour Me. By My Might, I shall make you taste the most painful chastisement.'"

According to a traditional report, Usama ibn Zaid (may Allah be well pleased with him and with his father) once heard Allah's Messenger (Allah bless him and give him peace) say:

A man will be cast into the Fire of Hell, so his guts will soon be dangling out of his belly. He will be rotated as a mill is rotated by its owner, and he will be asked: "Were you not in the habit of enjoining that which is right and fair [ma'ruf], and forbidding that which is wrong and unfair [munkar]?" To this he will reply: "I used to enjoin what is right and fair [ma'ruf], though I did not practice it myself, and I used to forbid is wrong and unfair [munkar], though I did not abstain from it myself."

The Prophet (Allah bless him and give him peace) once said:

Many a keeper of the fast [sa'im] receives nothing from his fasting [siyam] but hunger and thirst, and many a keeper of night vigil [qa'im] receives nothing from his vigil [qiyam] but insomnia.

To this the Prophet (Allah bless him and give him peace) added:

The Heavenly Throne ['Arsh] trembles because of that, and the Lord (Blessed and Exalted is He) is angry with him.

The Prophet (Allah bless him and give him peace) once said:

What a bad servant [of the Lord] is a servant who erects a barrier between himself and the spiritual reward of Allah (Exalted is He)! I am speaking of a servant, one of the creatures of Allah (Exalted is He), who devotes himself to His service, in the hope of receiving what He has at His disposal, and who exhausts his physical body in the effort to obtain His approval, but who makes a public show of his religious devotion [din], which is thereby rendered invalid.

His manly virtue [muru'a] degenerates into vice, and so he erects a barrier between himself and his Lord. He pins his hopes on Allah (Exalted is He), as far as the big picture is concerned, but he pins them on his fellow servant, when it comes to the small details. He gives some of his service to his fellow servant, at the expense of his worshipful obedience [ta'a] to Allah (Exalted is He).

Mujahid (may Allah bestow His mercy upon him) is reported as having said: "A man once came to Allah's Messenger (Allah bless him and give him peace) and said: 'O Messenger of Allah, I make it my practice to give charitable donations [atasaddaqu bi-sadaqa], so that I may obtain the gracious favour of Allah (Exalted is He). I also like to hear people speaking well of me.' At that very moment, His words (Blessed and Exalted is He):

So whoever hopes for the meeting with his Lord, let him do righteous work, and let him give no one any share at all in the worship due unto his Lord. (18:110)

--were sent down [to the Prophet (Allah bless him and give him peace)]." The Prophet (Allah bless him and give him peace) once said:

The end of the age will see the emergence of groups of people who exploit religion [din] for worldly purposes. To impress other people, they will dress in sheep's clothing, and their tongues will be sweeter than sugar, though their hearts are the hearts of wolves. Allah (Exalted is He) will say: "Are you deluding yourselves about Me, or are you so bold as to challenge Me deliberately?" I swear by Me, I shall surely inflict such confusion upon those people, that you would call the mildest case a case of utter bewilderment."

As we learn from a traditional report, Allah's Messenger (Allah bless him and give him peace) once said:

The angels will carry aloft the work of a certain servant from among the servants of Allah. They will multiply it and purify it, until they finally bring it to wherever Allah (Exalted is He) wishes it to be delivered, in all of His Dominion [Sultan]. Allah will thereupon convey to them, by way of inspiration: "You are custodians of My servant's work, while I am Ever-Watchful [Raqib] over what is in his soul [nafs]. This servant of Mine has not devoted his work sincerely to Me, so register him in the Deepest Pit [Sijjin]."

They will also rise aloft with the work of another servant from among His servants. They will diminish it and belittle it, until they finally bring it to wherever Allah (Exalted is He) wishes it to be delivered, in all of His Dominion [Sultan]. Allah will thereupon convey to them, by way of inspiration: "You are custodians of My servant's work, while I am Ever-Watchful [Raqib] over what is in his soul [nafs]. This servant of Mine has devoted his work sincerely to Me [akhlasa li 'amala-hu], so register him in the Highest Heaven ['Iliyyin]."

As reported on the authority of Abu Huraira (may Allah be well pleased with him), Allah's Messenger (Allah bless him and give him peace) once said:

On the Day of Resurrection [Yawm al-Qiyama], Allah (Blessed and Exalted is He) will judge between His creatures, while the members of every religious community [umma] fall on their knees. The first to be summoned will be a man who compiled a copy of the Qur'an, a man who was slain while fighting for Allah's cause [fi sabili'llah], and a man who possessed considerable wealth.

To the expert on the Qur'an [qari'], Allah (Exalted is He) will then say: "To what extent did you put what you learned into practice?" The man will reply: "I used to act upon it through the watches of the night, and at all times during the day." But Allah (Blessed and Exalted is He) will say: "You have told a lie!" The angels will also say: "You have told a lie! What you wanted, in fact, was to have people call you 'Qur'an-expert So-and so,' and you did indeed acquire that title."

The owner of wealth will be asked: "What did you do, to make good use of all that I made available to you?" The man will reply: "I was the source of compassion, and I applied it to charitable purposes." But Allah (Blessed and Exalted is He) will say: "You have told a lie!" The angels will also say: "You have told a lie! What you wanted, in fact, was to have people call you 'Generous Mister So-and-so,' and that was indeed how you came to be called."

The man who was slain while fighting for the cause of Allah (Exalted is He) will also be brought forward. To him Allah (Exalted is He) will say: "For what did you do battle?" The man will reply: "I fought for Your cause, until I was slain in Your cause." But Allah (Blessed and Exalted is He) will say: "You have told a lie!" The angels will also say: "You have told a lie! What you wanted, in fact, was to have people call you 'Brave Hero So-and-so,' and that was indeed how you came to be called."

At this point, Allah's Messenger (Allah bless him and give him peace) thumped his hands on his knees, and said:

"O Abu Huraira, on the Day of Resurrection [Yawm al-Qiyama], those three will be the first of the creatures of Allah (Almighty and Glorious is He) to be scorched by the Fire of Hell!"

Abu Huraira (may Allah be well pleased with him) also said: "This report came to the attention of Mu'awiya (may Allah be well pleased with him). On hearing it, he experienced an intense bout of weeping, then he said: 'Allah (Exalted is He) has spoken the truth, and His Messenger (Allah bless him and give him peace) has spoken the truth.' Then he recited these Qur'anic verses [ayat]:

As for those who desire the life of this world and its pomp, We shall repay them for their deeds therein, and therein they will not be wronged.

Such are those for whom there is nothing in the Hereafter but the Fire. All that they contrive here is vain, and all that they are used to doing is fruitless. (11:15,16)

Such are those for whom is the worst of torment, and in the Hereafter they will be among the greatest losers. (27:5)"

According to another traditional report, transmitted on the authority of 'Adi ibn Hatim at-Ta'i (may Allah be well pleased with him), Allah's Messenger (Allah bless him and give him peace) once said:

On the Day of Resurrection [Yawm al-Qiyama], the order will be given for some of those destined for the Fire of Hell to be herded toward the Garden of Paradise. They will be allowed to get close enough to smell its fragrant perfume, to view its palatial mansions, and to see what Allah (Exalted is He) has prepared for its inhabitants. Then they will hear the call: "Take them away! In this they have no share." So they will return whence they came, with a sense of distress and remorse, the like of which was never experienced by anyone making a return journey, in ancient or later times. They will say: "O our Lord, if only You had caused us to enter the Fire of Hell directly, before showing us what You have just shown us, meaning the reward You have prepared for those others!"

Allah (Exalted is He) will then say: "That is how I saw fit to treat you. When you were in private situations, you would brazenly affront Me with heinous sins ['aza'im], but when you met with other people, you would approach them modestly and humbly. By making a show of your deeds, you would give people an impression contrary to what was hidden away in your hearts. You were in awe of other people, but you did not regard Me with awe. You honoured other people, but you did not honour Me. You abstained, to please other people, from things you did not abandon for My sake. Today, therefore, I am giving you a taste of My painful chastisement, combined with a glimpse of My abundant reward, of which you have been deprived."

As reported on the authority of Ibn 'Abbas (may Allah be well pleased with him and with his father), Allah's Messenger (Allah bless him and give him peace) once said:

When Allah (Exalted is He) created the Garden of Eden [Jannat 'Adn], He created within it that which no eye has ever seen, of which no ear has ever heard, and the very notion of which has never occurred to the human heart. Then He said to it: "Speak to Me," and it responded by saying three times:

Successful indeed are the true believers. (23:1)

Then the Garden went on to say: "I am forbidden [haram] to every miser [bakhil] and ostentatious hypocrite [mura'i]."

A man once asked Allah's Messenger (Allah bless him and give him peace): "In what does salvation reside, tomorrow [at the Resurrection]?" He replied:

You must not try to deceive Allah (Exalted is He).

The man then asked: "How could I be guilty of trying to deceive Allah (Almighty and Glorious is He)?" The Prophet (Allah bless him and give him peace) explained:

By doing what He has commanded you to do, but doing it for some purpose other than to obtain the gracious favour of Allah (Exalted is He).

All of you must therefore beware of hypocritical display [riya'], for it is tantamount to associating partners [shirk] with Allah (Exalted is He). Indeed, on the Day of Resurrection [Yawm al-Qiyama], the ostentatious hyprocrite [mura'i] will be summoned by four names, over the heads of all the assembled creatures: "O unbeliever [ya kafir]! O shameless liar [ya fajir]! O traitor [ya ghadir]! O loser [ya khasir]! Your work has gone astray, and your recompense has been cancelled, so there is no share for you here today. Apply for your wages to those for whom you used to work, O deceiver!" Let us therefore take refuge with Allah (Almighty and Glorious is He) from hypocritical display [riya'], from promoting an undeserved reputation [sum'a], and from hypocrisy itself [nifaq], for that is the work of those who are doomed to the Fire of Hell. Allah (Almighty and Glorious is He) has said:

Surely the hypocrites will be in the lowest depth of the Fire [of Hell]. (4:145)

In other words, they will be in the Pit [al-Hawiya], in the company of Pharaoh [Fir'awn] and Haman and their people. As someone might well see fit to interject at this point, it seems be suggested, in at least one of the traditional reports [akhbar], that there is actually no harm in having our religious practice noticed by our fellow creatures. According to the report in question, it was Abu Huraira (may Allah be well pleased with him) who said: "A man came to Allah's Messenger (Allah bless him and give him peace) and said: 'O Messenger of Allah, I perform my religious practice, intending to keep it private, but I find that people are watching, and that pleases me. If such be the case, am I entitled to any reward?' To this he replied (Allah bless him and give him peace):

'You are entitled to two rewards: the reward for the secrecy, and the reward for the publicity.'"

To resolve what may appear to be a contradiction, this should be construed as follows: What made that man feel pleased, was the fact that people followed the example he was setting, in the performance of his religious practice. Allah's Messenger (Allah bless him and give him peace) was aware of this, so he told the man, in effect: "You are entitled to two rewards: one reward for your righteous work, and one reward for having people follow your good example." As he once said (Allah bless him and give him peace):

If someone establishes a good custom [sanna sunnatan hasana], he is entitled to the reward for it, and also to the reward of all those who practice it, until the Day of Resurrection [Yawm al-Qiyama].

On the other hand, if someone enjoys the pleasing sensation in and of itself, and not on account of the good example he is setting for others, he is not entitled to any reward, because vain conceit ['ujb] can only cause the servant to fall from grace in the sight of Allah. It was al-Hasan al-Basri (may Allah bestow His mercy upon him) who said: "If you wish, you may choose a companion with a fair complexion, but with crude manners, one who has a smooth tongue and a sharp eye, but who is dead at heart. You see physical bodies, not hearts. You listen to the sound of music, but not to a close friend. Tongues have grown fertile, while hearts have turned barren. As a matter of fact, several Companions [Ashab] of Allah's Messenger (Allah bless him and give him peace) have told me that this Community [Umma] will remain beneath the hand of Allah, in His protective custody, but only as long as its Qur'an-reciters [qurra'] and its commanders [umara'] do not lose interest in their work, as long as its honest members [sulaha'] do not join the ranks of the lying scoundrels [fujjar], and as long as its best representatives keep the worst at bay. As soon as they reverse their positions, Allah (Exalted is He) will remove His protecting hand from them. He will smite them with poverty and want. He will fill their hearts with terror, and He will subject them to the rule of tyrants [jababira], who will make them suffer dreadful torment." He [al-Hasan al-Basri (may Allah bestow His mercy upon him)] also said: "What a bad servant [of the Lord] is he! I am speaking of a servant who fits the following description:

* He asks for forgiveness [maghfira], while he is actively engaged in sinful disobedience [ma'siya].

* He behaves in a humbly submissive manner, so that he may be credited with loyalty [amana], but he is only pretending, to hide his disloyalty [khiyana].

* He forbids what is wrong, but does not refrain from it himself [yanha wa la yantahi].

* He enjoins what is right, but does not act upon his own instructions.

* If he gives, he does so very stingily, and if he withholds, he offers no apology.

* If he is in the best of health, he feels secure, but if he falls sick, he becomes remorseful.

* If he is impoverished, he feels sad, and if he gets rich, he is subject to temptation.

* He hopes for salvation, but does not act accordingly.

* He is afraid of punishment, but takes no precautions against it.

* He wishes to receive more benefit, but he does not give thanks [for what he has received].

* He likes the idea of spiritual reward, but he does not practice patience.

* He expedites sleep [nawm], and postpones fasting [sawm]."

He [al-Hasan al-Basri (may Allah bestow His mercy upon him)] spoke one day to Farqad as-Sabakhi, who was sitting in attendance at his meeting [majlis]. In sharp contrast to al-Hasan, who was dressed in very smart attire, Farqad was wearing a jubba made of wool [suf]. "My clothing," said al-Hasan, "is the clothing of the people of the Garden of Paradise, while your clothing is the clothing of the people of the Fire of Hell. They lodge their pious abstinence [zuhd] in their clothing, and their arrogant pride in their breasts. By Allah, any one of them is far more conceited about his wool [suf] than a fashionable shawl-designer is about his fancy shawl. What is wrong with competing together in excellence? Why not dress outwardly in the style of kings, and kill your hearts with fear [of displeasing the Lord]?"

'Umar [ibn al-Khattab] (may Allah be well pleased with him) once said: "You should dress in a style that will neither cause the Qur'an-reciters [qurra'] to treat you as a laughingstock, nor make silly idiots deride you."

As they used to say: "Be woollen [sufi] at heart, and cotton-made [qutni] in clothing." To put the subject in a nutshell, the people [who matter to us] fall into three categories, where clothing is concerned: (1) the devout [atqiya'], (2) the saints [awliya'], and (3) the spiritual deputies [abdal].

* The clothing of the devout [atqiya'] is that which is lawful [halal], in the sense that none of the wearer's fellow creatures have any claim on it, and that it does not violate the sacred law [shar'] in any respect. As for whether their clothes are of

cotton [qutn] or wool [suf], and whether they are white or blue, that is neither here not there.

* The clothing of the saints [awliya'] is determined by the [divine] commandment. At the very least, it must be sufficient to cover the genital area ['awra], and any other part of the body for which it is essential. Some form of clothing is called for, of necessity, to ensure the discouragement of their passionate desires, so that they may attain to the degree of the spiritual deputies [abdal].

* The clothing of the spiritual deputies [budala'] is whatever destiny [qadar] brings to the individual concerned, always with due respect to the limits set by the sacred law [hudud]. It may be a plain shirt worth a mere qirat [one twentieth of a dinar], or a fine suit worth a hundred dinars [gold coins], for there is no self-will involved. They have ascended to the highest height, and there is no passionate desire to be discouraged at the lowest level. For them, it is simply a matter of accepting whatever the Master [Mawla] graciously confers, whatever He allows and bestows, without trouble or concern, and without respect for the lower self [nafs] and personal preferences. Aside from these perspectives, any other approach to the subject can be traced to the ancient Time of Ignorance [Jahiliyya], to the frivolous inclination of the lower self [nafs], and to the influence of passionate desire [hawa].

******